WHAT IS PROTEIN COMPLEMENTARITY?

The combination, in the proper proportions, of non-meat foods, that produces high-grade protein nutrition equivalent to—or *better than*—meat proteins.

AND THAT IS WHAT THIS BOOK IS ALL ABOUT

From the Foreword:

This book is about protein—how we as a nation are caught in a pattern that squanders it: and how you can choose the opposite—a way of eating that makes the most of the earth's capacity to supply this vital nutrient.

The world has come a long way toward recognizing some of its problems in the last few years. No final solutions have been found, but a trend that has been realized and acknowledged—at least on the part of young people— is the movement away from waste, away from heavily polluted foods.

The concepts in this book are no final solution either. But they represent a giant step in the right direction. For the first time it is possible to implement an end to the gross waste of literally millions of tons of high-grade protein, to release men from the confines of a largely meat diet, to enjoy nutritionally sound protein from the richer and far more abundant sources that the earth provides. Here, step by step, is how you, the individual, can improve your own style-of-life—and at the same time help your very small planet.

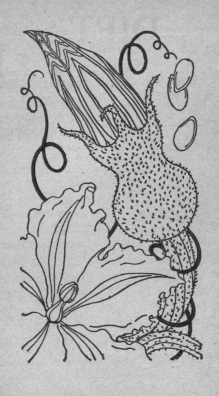

OTHER BALLANTINE BOOKS
YOU WILL ENJOY

DIET
FOR A SMALL
PLANET

Frances Moore Lappé

Illustrated
by
Kathleen Zimmerman
and
Ralph Iwamoto

A FRIENDS OF THE EARTH / BALLANTINE BOOK

NEW YORK

Copyright © 1971 by Frances Moore Lappé

All rights reserved.

SBN 345-02378-1-125

First Printing: September, 1971
Second Printing: November, 1971
Third Printing: May, 1972
Fourth Printing: July, 1972
Fifth Printing: December, 1972
Sixth Printing: February, 1973
Seventh Printing: April, 1973

Printed in the United States of America

Cover art by Charles Fracé

BALLANTINE BOOKS, INC.
101 Fifth Avenue, New York, N.Y. 10003

Contents

Appendices

Acknowledgments

The fun of writing this book was increased immeas-
urably by the aid and encouragement of friends. First
I must thank the person who created the delicious dinner
that introduced me to the pleasures of eating without
meat—Ellen Ewald. After dinner I went through her
kitchen asking: What's this? What's that? And she sent
me home with a variety of samples—soy grits, whole
oats, buckwheat groats, bulgur—all these strange
sounding foods which are really among the most common foods in the world! Ellen is also the person you
can thank for many of the appetizing recipes you'll find
later in the book. Her help made compiling the recipes
an adventure.

I wish to thank my husband, Marc, for his constant
encouragement and creative touch just as I would reach
an impasse. Without his faith in me, I'm sure I would
never have attempted, much less completed, this task!
Several other good friends have taken much time and
thought to give editorial criticism and counsel: Lloyd
Linford, Walter Meagher, Marion Abzug, and Doro-
thy and Paul Shields. Sally Rehwald and Susan Cun-
ningham contributed willingly of their artistic talents for
the early draft of the book. The support of these friends
made the project totally satisfying at every stage—not
merely when it was finally done. Last I wish to thank
my parents, John and Ina Moore, who, by having always
set the finest example of critical openness to new ideas,
made this inquiry possible.

Oats

Foreword

This book is about PROTEIN—how we as a nation are caught in a pattern that squanders it; and how you can choose the opposite—a way of eating that makes the most of the earth's capacity to supply this vital nutrient. In the pages that follow I propose that our heavily meat-centered culture is at the very heart of our waste of the earth's productivity; and I invite you to explore the varied possibilities of nonmeat sources of protein.

Why has the information I have gathered not been easily available long before now? And why now is it being presented by someone who is neither a nutritionist nor an ecologist? Perhaps the answer is that we have neglected vital questions because of fixed cultural attitudes which relegate nonmeat protein sources to an inferior position. The fact that the first comprehensive research in plant protein became available only six months ago illustrates this meat-centered bias. As you are reading, you may discover that many of your beliefs about protein have been culturally conditioned. I know that mine were, and that just getting the facts has been marvelously freeing. When a meal was no longer rigidly defined as meat-vegetable-potatoes, many new and exciting culinary experiences became possible.

So that you can understand my perspective, I want to share with you how I came to write this book.

Several years ago I became intrigued with the debate

over the "world food problem." In a world where the majority is hungry, there seemed to me no more urgent question. According to the books I read at that time, man was reaching the very limits of the earth's capacity to produce food. Although there was much disagreement about alternatives for expanding the earth's capacity, the focus was always clear: *it was the earth's natural limitations that man had to worry about.*

Naively I set out to determine for myself just how near the "limit" we were. Although, of course, I failed, the venture did pay off: my assumptions were severely jolted. First, I was astounded by how little of the earth's surface is really well suited to producing food.

I had always assumed that only three elements were needed for agriculture: sun, water, and soil. And since these elements are almost omnipresent on the planet, I thought that agricultural potential must also be. Then I realized that we probably came to hold this distorted view because all we know is our own country. But how exceptional America is! We are endowed with *all* the complex requirements for high agricultural productivity, more so than any other nation in the world.

At about the same time I came across the fact that a very large portion of these superb agricultural resources are funneled into the production of meat. I wondered whether this was really the most productive use of our rich agricultural land.

Suddenly I began to see the world's problems with food as my point of reference. Other facts began to strike me that I had previously taken for granted. I thought about products like coffee and tea. Don't they grow on agricultural land, land that might otherwise be growing nutritious food? Why do these patterns of land use exist if man needs food, and good land is scarce?

All this went through my mind. The questions I had originally asked with such a sense of urgency began to fade in importance. I now saw that in a world where only a minor portion of the land is really well suited to agriculture, man is using much of the best land with dubious efficiency. And I saw that much agricultural land which might be growing food is being used instead to "grow" money (in the form of coffee, tea, etc.). But all this had nothing to do with the earth's *natural* limits, the issue that at first had so concerned me. Maybe, I finally concluded, instead of studying geography to understand the earth's food-producing potential, I should be examining what man is doing with the food he *presently* produces. This decision resulted in Part 1—a probing of the protein waste built into our present meat-oriented culture.

But if I had hopes of evaluating the wisdom of our concentration on meat production, I would have to know a lot about protein. Everyone knows we need protein and that we get protein from meat. But might there be other good protein sources that could be produced with less waste? What about plants? Even a Commission of the National Academy of Sciences of this country has concluded that to survive in the future we will all have to rely more on plants and less on meat for protein. Certainly then we want to know just how plants can meet human needs for protein.

Thus, the nutritional value of plants—their advantages and limitations—took on new interest for me. I searched at length for some relatively simple explanation of the viability of a nonmeat diet for humans. I could find none. I was shocked: after all, haven't there always been vegetarians, and aren't there presently millions of people eating a nonmeat diet either by choice or necessity?

I was amazed to learn that much of the critical study of plant protein is just now beginning to be done. For this reason, only now is it possible to leave behind the practically useless protein "guides" which purport to give the "amount" of protein in foods. In any food only a portion of the protein is actually usable by the body. Rather than merely stating the amount of protein in the food, I discovered that the only meaningful way to present protein data is in a form that relates this *usable* protein to your daily protein needs. This is what Parts II and III are all about. They are designed as a guide for making the most of plant protein, thus opening up for you a nutritionally sound alternative to a meat-centered diet.

Some will find little value in my thesis on the grounds that it doesn't offer a practical guide for solving the world's food problems. But reestablishing a sense of our direct impact on the earth through food may be the first step toward changing our cultural pattern of waste. However, I'll have to admit that the appeal to me has been more to my feelings than my rationality. First, it has to do with the tremendous personal satisfaction of being able to make real choices; indeed, how rare this is! Previously, when I went to a supermarket, I felt at the mercy of our advertising culture. My tastes were manipulated. And food, instead of being my most direct link with the nurturing earth, had become mere merchandise by which I fulfilled my role as a "good" consumer. But as I gained the understanding that I have tried to communicate to you in this book, I found that I *was* making choices, choices based on real knowledge about food and about the effect on the earth of different types of food production. It was a gradual process in which there was no question of a sacrifice in giving up meat. Rather, as new types of food combinations became more attractive, shopping for food and cooking was no longer unconscious and boring, but a real adventure. The adventure was the discovery of ways, the best, most delicious ways, of making the most of the earth's productivity.

Diet for a Small Planet

Part I

Earth's Labor
Lost

Two kinds of Millet
Hungarian Grass and Broomcorn (common) Millet

WHEN YOUR MOTHER told you to eat everything on your plate because people were starving in India, you thought it was pretty silly. You knew that the family dog would be the only one affected by what you did or didn't waste. Since then you've probably continued to think that making any sort of *ethical* issue about eating is absurd. You eat what your family always ate, altered only perhaps by proddings from the food industry. It's probably a pretty unconscious affair, and you like it that way. But eating habits can have a meaning, a meaning that not only feels closer to you than an abstract ethic but brings you pleasure too. What I am about to describe to you may sound at first like just another ethical rule for eating, but to me it feels like common sense far removed from the abstract.

The act of putting into your mouth what the earth has grown is perhaps your most direct interaction with the earth. But, depending on the eating habits of a culture, this interaction can have very different consequences—for mankind, and for the earth. What I will be suggesting in this book is a guideline for eating from the earth that both maximizes the earth's potential to meet man's nutritional needs and, at the same time, minimizes the disruption of the earth necessary to sustain him. It's as simple as that.

In order to understand this very simple idea of making the most of the earth's productivity while doing the least damage, we must have a clear picture of our present practices and their consequences. Since the eating habits of this culture center so heavily on meat, the best place to start is with the United States livestock production.

Cows

A. A Protein Factory in Reverse

Think for a moment of a cow grazing. We see the cow as one link in a food chain of which man is the last link. Man is, therefore, the obvious beneficiary. The cow eats grass and we get steak. What could be a better arrangement! But before we acclaim our good fortune let's examine just how the conversion of plants to meat occurs in practice. You will see that in this country we have drastically altered this simple grass-to-meat equation.

Livestock could very well serve man as a "protein factory," converting humanly inedible substances, like cellulose, and low-quality protein in plants into high-quality protein for our benefit. Grazing livestock on rangeland of little agricultural value is clearly fulfilling this function. And, as we shall see later, some livestock can even produce protein with a diet based on as simple a molecule as urea!

The President's Science Advisory Committee believes that livestock "protein factories" are, in fact, operating primarily to turn humanly unusable nutrients into foodstuffs for man. In the mammoth report entitled *The World Food Problem,* they emphasize that:

> The use of *small* quantities of cereal grains as livestock feed in modern nations makes it possible to use, at *low* cost in terms of food that could be consumed by people, large quantities of forages and by-products that might not be used otherwise. (*Emphasis added.*) [1]

Unfortunately, this ideal arrangement is simply not realized. Relatively little advantage is actually made of the ability of livestock to convert inedible and low-quality material into high-quality human food in this and other highly industrialized countries. On the contrary, *enormous* quantities of the *highest*-quality food sources are fed to animals.

Fully *one-half* of the harvested agricultural land in the U.S. is planted with feed crops.[2] We feed 78 percent of all our grain to animals. This is the largest percentage of any country in the world. In Russia, 28 percent of grains are fed to animals,* while in developing countries, the percentage ranges from 10 to *0.*[3]

Converted into protein these statistics mean that in

---

* Note that the Russian diet has about the same amount of total protein as the American diet. (Based on protein availability statistics.)

1968 U.S. livestock (minus dairy cows) were fed *20 million tons of protein primarily from sources that could be eaten directly by man*.[4] Cattle and hogs alone accounted for one-half of the total protein consumed. This figure is minimal in that it excludes protein from alfalfa, hay, and low-grade by-product feeds.† It *does* include the protein from most of our domestically used grains, specifically: 89 percent of our corn crop, 98 percent of our grain sorghum crop,‡ 87 percent of our oat crop, 64 percent of our barley crop,[5] as well as 95 percent of our unexported soybean crop,[6] and a significant portion of the wheat and rye harvest. In addition, this 20 million tons of protein include about 950,000 tons of fish products fed to American livestock in 1968.[7]

But these figures acquire real meaning only when we take into account the efficiency of livestock in the conversion of "feed" into protein for us. It is widely accepted that the ratio of nutrients put into an animal to the nutrients recovered for human consumption is high. For example, the protein production ratio for beef and veal in North America is 21 to 1. This means that a cow must be fed 21 pounds of protein in order to produce 1 pound of protein for human consumption. Other types of animal protein conversion are somewhat more efficient. Chart I shows how they compare.[8]

Considering all classes of livestock in the U.S., the average ratio of protein conversion is 8 to 1.[9]

Another way of assessing the relative inefficiency of livestock is by comparison with plants in the amount of protein produced per acre. An acre of cereals can produce *five times* more protein than an acre devoted to

† One by-product fed to animals which is not so "low grade" is the high-quality protein products (e.g., wheat germ) left over after making white flour.

‡ Grain sorghum is not eaten here but is a staple in many parts of Africa and elsewhere.

CHART I
LIVESTOCK PROTEIN CONVERSION EFFICIENCY

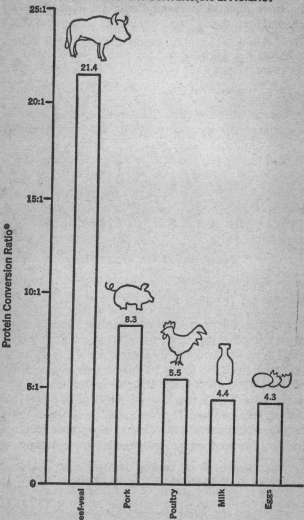

*No. of lbs. protein fed livestock to produce 1 lb. protein for human consumption.

meat production; legumes (peas, beans, lentils) can produce *ten times* more; and leafy vegetables *fifteen times*
more. These figures are averages—some plants in each
category actually produce even more. Spinach, for example, can produce up to twenty-six times more protein
per acre than can beef.[10]

Barley, Rye, Millet, Oats, Wheat

Now let us put these two factors together: the large
quantities of humanly edible protein being fed to animals, and their inefficient conversion into protein for
human consumption. Some very startling statistics result.
If we exclude dairy cows, the average ratio for protein
conversion by livestock in North America is 10 to 1.
Applying this ratio to the 20 million tons of protein fed
to livestock in 1968 in the U.S., we realize that only 10
percent (or 2 million tons) was retrieved as protein for
human consumption. Thus, in a single year through this
consumption pattern, 18 million tons of protein becomes
inaccessible to man.* This amount is equivalent to

---

* The mention of yet another "cost" of meat production
should not be neglected in a world where all our natural resources are becoming scarce. C. C. Bradley estimates in an
article in *Science* that to produce a beef and grain based diet
requires about eight times as much *water* as a diet based solely
on grains.[11]

90 percent of the yearly world protein deficit[12]—enough protein to provide 12 grams a day for every person in the world!

The Dean of Agriculture of Ohio State University has estimated that 40 percent of world livestock production is derived from vegetable sources suitable for human food. If made available to man directly, he concludes, the world food supply could be increased by 35 percent.[13] And, according to Don Paarlberg, a former U.S. Assistant Secretary of Agriculture, just reducing our livestock population by one-half would release about 100 million tons of grains for human consumption.[14] (This amount would meet the caloric deficit of the "nonsocialist" developing countries almost *four times over.*[15])

But perhaps the most revealing statement about the way the rich West uses its productive capacity is that of Lyle P. Schertz, an administrator in the U.S. Department of Agriculture, in the June, 1971 issue of *War on Hunger*: ". . . the billion people in the developed countries use practically as much cereals as *feed* to produce animal protein as the two billion people of the developing countries use directly as *food*." (emphasis added)

That our current level of protein waste can be compared to the world protein deficit is staggering. But the waste of our food resources appears even more grievous in light of the existence of malnutrition in this country. The tragic irony is well stated by Senator Ernest Hollings in his recent book, *The Case Against Hunger*[16]: "With our U.S. Department of Agriculture setting the rules, we no longer allow farmers to give their livestock and poultry anything but the best formulated feeds. . . . Yet millions of American human beings are hungry, and the early scientific indications are that general nutrition in this country is worse than it was at the close of World War II."

In his book Senator Hollings reports results from the National Nutrition Survey whose director, Dr. Arnold Schaefer, has stated that the nutrition problems among the poor in the United States "seem to be similar to those we have encountered in the developing countries." The two most serious nutritional diseases, are kwashiorkor, caused by severe, long-term protein deficiency, and marasmus which results primarily from prolonged lack of food calories. (You may recall seeing pictures of starving Biafran children whose bodies were misshapen from starvation. They were suffering from these diseases.) "Both," Senator Hollings points out, "are rare exceptions except in famine conditions. But both were found by doctors of the nutrition survey, here in our great and bounteous land."

Early samplings of the National Nutrition Survey (undertaken by the Department of Health, Education and Welfare) in which half the families earned less than $3000 a year showed that more than 16 percent had serious protein deficiencies—some well below the levels normally associated with malnutrition in underdeveloped countries. Bone underdevelopment and swollen bellies due to protein or calorie malnutrition were observed in 4 to 5 percent. This data was gathered in Texas and Louisiana. Cases of marasmus were found in Nashville, Tennessee, and both kwashiorkor and marasmus were identified in the U.S. Public Health Hospital on an Indian reservation in Arizona. As Dr. Schaefer quietly put it, "We did not expect to find such cases in the United States."

The reason I am able to give you only preliminary data is that the National Nutrition Survey, originally intended to be nationwide, was curtailed in 1970 before an analysis of even the first ten-state study could be completed. Senator Hollings reasons that the early results of the survey were "politically embarrassing" to the Nixon administration. So this is where we stand: unwilling even to register the extent of this country's failure to use its unparalleled agricultural capacity to provide healthy diets for its people.

B. The Fatted Calf

It is astonishing that, although protein is a precious commodity in most parts of the world, Americans actually place a higher value on fat. The purpose of the high-protein feeds is *not* primarily to produce a high-protein carcass, as one would assume. On the contrary, when cattle are fed in the 120 to 150 days before slaughter, the purpose is to fatten up or "finish" (as cattle men say) the animal. The higher the fat content of the meat, the higher the animal is graded—prime grade being the fattiest, and choice grade next. Choice grade beef, for example, trimmed to retail level, has about 63 percent more fat than standard grade.

One reason we use high-protein feeds to produce fat is that the meat taste to which we are accustomed results in part from the fat content. But we don't know the minimum level of protein concentrate feeding consistent with our definition of "good taste." In fact, we continue to *increase* the level of high-protein feeding. (Though I've heard no one complaining that steaks don't taste good enough!) The pressure to use high-protein feeds is mounting. According to James Clawson, an animal scientist at the University of California, Davis, a cow may now be fed these concentrates for up to two-thirds of its life. Why? Well, Mr. Clawson states, the pressure is economic. It's more profitable to feed a high-protein diet than a largely roughage diet for two reasons. First, when the greatest profit is derived from the highest turnover of livestock, the producer will prefer the shortest possible feeding method, i.e., a high-protein diet. Second, a roughage diet requires grazing land and, he asserts, land prices are prohibitively high. Thus, as the land prices go up, so does the pressure to turn to high-protein concentrates.[17]

Even if fat were as valuable nutritionally as protein, our present practices would be wasteful. You see, there's no way to insure that the extra fat put on the animal will be internal fat, marbled in the meat; it can also be external fat that is trimmed away. We feed and grade for the highest fat content despite the fact that today's beef carcass is one-fifth fat, swine is one-fourth fat, and lamb is one-third fat.[18] Much of this, of course, is thrown away. The rest becomes part of an interesting trade pattern in which the U.S. comes out decidedly on top. For example, in 1968 Peru and Chile shipped to the U.S. about 700,000 tons of high-protein fish products which we fed to animals.[19] And what was the major U.S. agricultural export to Peru? Twenty-six thousand pounds of inedible tallow and grease![20]

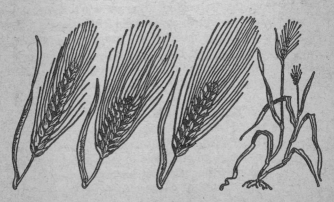

Barley

C. The Hidden Talent of Livestock

Nothing inherent in livestock production requires this enormous waste of protein. Potentially, livestock *can* function as "protein factories"; they just aren't given a chance to do so! Already, livestock convert land of marginal fertility unsuited for crops into meat for man. In fact, between one-third and one-half of the continental land surface is used for grazing.[21] This is one of those staggering figures that leaves one incredulous. I did not believe it until I verified the estimate in the original Department of Agriculture source. It then became one of the first facts which motivated me to pursue the research for this book.

But the biology of ruminants is more remarkable than this figure would indicate. Animals like cattle, sheep, and goats don't need to *eat* protein to *produce* protein. Microorganisms in the stomachs of ruminants can convert nitrogen, in the form of urea, into protein. Dairy cows, for example, have produced up to 4235 kilograms of milk a year containing 164 kilograms of protein, on a diet of urea, ammonium salts, potato starch, cellulose, and sucrose, without any other source of protein. *Many cows on the standard U.S. high-protein diet do no better!* And the vitamin and mineral content of the "deprived cows'" milk was normal.[22] In another study a beef calf weighing 290 pounds was given urea as its only source of protein. The calf more than tripled its weight and when grown gave birth to a healthy offspring.[23]

As the President's Science Advisory Committee points out, the only reason more urea (humanly inedible) is not used as animal feed is that grains (humanly edible) are available at low prices. The reason, of course, for the low price of grain is the limited "demand." Of course, real demand exists in terms of human need but hungry people are by definition unable to express this demand. Traditional dollar values obviously have little to do with human needs.

D. The U.S. Protein Sink

Not only do our agricultural practices waste domestic protein resources, but America also puts into her "protein sink" meat and feed of underdeveloped countries. In 1968, we imported 332 million pounds of meat from Latin America—much of it coming from the poorest areas of Central America.[24] At least 20 percent of this meat is protein, enough to provide 60 grams of protein per day for an entire year to 1.4 million people, or most of the population of a country like Costa Rica.

Ironically, the U.S. Agency for International Development is willing to provide up to $40,000 for an American company to go into Central America to see whether or not they can make a profit by selling novel high-protein food supplements to the hungry peasants.[25] At the same time this area exports about 100 million tons of meat to us and we play an important role in determining that much of their land is used to make money for a few, not food for the people.

In 1968, we imported primarily from Chile and Peru 700,000 tons of fishmeal for use as feed.[26] There is enough protein in this quantity of fishmeal to supply 15 million people—more than the whole population of Peru—with protein for a year. In fact, according to an official of the Food and Agriculture Organization of the U.N., half of the world fish catch in 1968 was fed to livestock![27] Some try to rationalize such practice on the grounds that native populations find the fishmeal unpalatable. But, considering the many possibilities for treating fishmeal and adding it as a tasteless protein concentrate to popular local foods, this is hardly an excuse.

In any case, the *last* place that the fishmeal should end up is the stomachs of American livestock!

E. Wasting the Waste

Some people believe that although we do feed enormous quantities of high-grade protein nutrients to livestock with relatively little return as food for humans, there is really no loss. After all, we live in a closed system. Animal waste returns to the soil, providing nutrients for the crops that the animals themselves will eventually eat—thus completing a natural ecological cycle. If this were only true!

Animal waste in the U.S. amounts to 2.0 billion tons annually, equivalent to the waste of 2.0 billion people, or more than half of the world's population.[28] What a Herculean task it would be to collect and distribute this quantity of animal waste in order to complete our idealized ecological cycle! In contrast to the agricultural practices of other countries, conditions of livestock production in the U.S. completely mitigate against any such possibility. Concentration of from 10,000 to 50,000 animals (and up to 250,000 poultry) in a single feedlot

Green pepper, Scallions, Mushrooms, Garlic

results in a surfeit of potential fertilizer far exceeding the capacity of the surrounding farmland. And, since it is not economical to transport the waste to where it might be used, most of the waste finds its way into our water systems. This leads to depletion of oxygen, encourages eutrophication, and contaminates the water with pathogens. Thus, as you can see, the ecological cycle is not able to complete itself and even the waste is wasted!

F. Land That Grows Money Can't Grow Food

So far I have concentrated on the loss of nutrients through livestock production. But I'd also like to mention another misuse of the earth's productive potential for which the West must bear responsibility.

Beginning over 300 years ago the wealthy Western powers established the plantation system in their subject lands. The plantation's sole purpose was to produce wealth for the colonizers, not food for men. Thus, most of the crops selected by the colonizers—tobacco, rubber, tea, coffee, cocoa, cotton, and other fibers—have negligible nutritional value. The name subsequently given to them, "cash crops," is quite an appropriate label.

Cash crops became established in world trade as the only proper exports from the Third World; so that even after emancipation from formal colonial control, Third World countries were economically "hooked" on cash crops as their only means of survival. Coffee alone is the economic lifeblood of *forty* developing countries— as in the African country of Rwanda, where coffee represents 87.5 percent of earnings from foreign exchange.

Obviously cash crops usurp land, often the best

agricultural land, that could be growing food for an undernourished local population. Over 250,000 square miles are presently planted with nonnutritious cash crops[29]*—more than one and one-half times the entire area of California and equal to two-thirds of all the arable land in Latin America. And, more land is put under the system every day. The Food and Agriculture Organization of the U.N. reports that *nonedible* agricultural production is growing at a faster rate than edible food production in the developing countries.[80]

The rich West points to the demands of international trade as the reason for the bind in which the Third World finds itself. True enough. But the real question remains unanswered: who is responsible for creating this pattern of land use and the subsequent rules of international trade?

G. Mining the Soil

But let us for a moment accept the rules of the economic game. Then, since the U.S. can "afford" this waste of protein, why not indulge ourselves? Why not continue our inefficient livestock production and heavy importation of protein until such time as the pressure of our own population or political changes abroad force us to use our resources more wisely?

This reasoning assumes that the only cost of our present indulgence is wasted protein which at any moment could be retrieved. But in reality our productive capacity hinges on the quality of our soil which, if lost, cannot so readily be regained. Our heavy use of agricultural land depletes the soil and results in lower-quality agricultural

---

* Includes only rubber, coffee, tobacco, cocoa, tea, cotton, and other fibers. Other cash crops from which the local population receives little nutritional benefit include bananas and sugar.

output. For example in 1940 it was quite common for Kansas wheat to be as much as 17 percent protein. By 1951, only *eleven* years later, no Kansas wheat had over 14 percent protein, most being between 11 and 12 percent.[31]

Georg Borgstrom, nutritionist, geographer, and the author of two outstanding books* on the world's food supply, decries the fact that in many parts of the world "overgrazing and excessive ploughing have . . . paved the way for the destructive forces of soil erosion. It is well documented," he states, "that the United States has lost one-fourth of its topsoil since the prairies were first broken by the plough."[32] But what necessitates this intense use of the soil that precludes its natural self-renewal? The source of the "pressure" becomes apparent if we recall that half of the harvest in the U.S. each year goes to livestock.

One factor that has allowed us to push the limits of the soil's productive capacity is pesticides. Let's see how they get into our diet and pertain to the main theme of the book.

Rice and Legumes

---

* *The Hungry Planet* and *Too Many*.

H. Eating Low on the Food Chain

By now most of us are familiar with the facts of environmental damage wrought by chlorinated pesticides like DDT: in predatory birds like pelicans and falcons, DDT and related pesticides like Dieldrin can disrupt reproductive processes, and in ocean-going fish like salmon, DDT can cause damage to the nervous system. What may be less familiar to you, and of greater importance to us here, is just *why* these particular species are being affected. A major reason is that these animals are at the top of long food chains in which pesticides accumulate as one organism is eaten by another. This process of accumulation results from the fact that organochlorine pesticides like DDT and Dieldrin are retained in animal and fish fat and are difficult to break down. Thus, as big fish eat smaller fish, or as cows eat grass (or feed), whatever pesticides they eat are largely retained and passed on. So if man is eating at the "top" of such food chains, he becomes the final consumer and thus the recipient of the highest concentration of pesticide residues.

But unlike most other predators (or "carnivores," if you like), man has a choice of what and how much he eats. We have already explored one of the reasons for choosing to be an "herbivore" that eats low on the food chain—it is simply less wasteful. Another consideration, the one we are going to evaluate here, is that herbivores are less likely to accumulate potentially harmful environmental contaminants than are carnivores.

Now, the Food and Drug Administration of this country knows its ecology as well or better than we do, and they have taken pains to keep pesticides out of the diets of the animals and animal products that we consume. Indeed, there are exceedingly few feed products for which the FDA has authorized pesticide spraying. In particular, they have scrupulously prevented the spraying of alfalfa with chlorinated pesticides like DDT. Does this mean that our concern about food chain concentration of contaminants is unfounded?

Marc Lappé, my husband, who is an experimental pathologist interested in the problem of environmental contamination, has pulled together the information necessary to answer our query. He turned to an important new scientific journal devoted exclusively to monitoring the levels of pesticides in the American environment, *The Pesticides Monitoring Journal.* In 1969, this journal included an extensive study of the pesticide residues in the American diet. Between 1964 and 1968 the principal types of pesticide residues found (about 85%) were chlorinated pesticides like DDT.* In a summary report given in 1969, two principal investigators of pesticide contamination in the U.S. diet reached the following conclusion: "Foods of animal origin continue to be the major source of chlorinated organic pesticidal residues in the diet."[33]

They note that this is true *in spite* of the fact that food categories like dairy products, meat, fish, and poultry received little if any direct application of pesticides during the period when monitoring was done. Thus, the "precautions" taken to avoid beef contamination with pesticide residues have actually proven to be ecologically meaningless. Apparently, most of the residues were coming from indirect sources in the environment.

The accompanying bar graph, Chart II, shows you in summary form the kind of data on which these researchers relied. The bars indicate parts of chlorinated pesticides per million parts of food (parts per million, or ppm). Note that meat, fish, and poultry contain two-and-a-half times more chlorinated pesticides than the second-place dairy products, but about thirteen times more than

---

* DDT and its breakdown products DDE and TDE accounted for over two-thirds of the total organochlorine residues.

CHART II

SOURCES OF PESTICIDE RESIDUES IN THE U.S. DIET

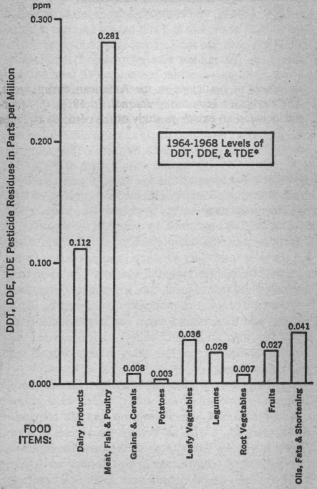

ppm

0.300

0.281

0.200

1964-1968 Levels of
DDT, DDE, & TDE°

0.112

0.100

0.000

0.008   0.003   0.036   0.026   0.007   0.027   0.041

DDT, DDE, TDE Pesticide Residues in Parts per Million

FOOD
ITEMS:

Dairy Products

Meat, Fish & Poultry

Grains & Cereals

Potatoes

Leafy Vegetables

Legumes

Root Vegetables

Fruits

Oils, Fats & Shortening

Source: Calculated from data presented in P. E. Cornellussen, "Pesticide Residues in Total Diet Sample (IV)", *Pesticides Monitoring Journal*
(2:140-152, 1969).

°Averages of combined data from five American cities: Boston, Kansas
City, Los Angeles, Baltimore and Minneapolis.

the average level of the remaining seven groups. This means that if you eliminated meat, fish, and poultry entirely from your diet and replaced them with plant sources of protein, you could *triple* your intake of vegetable sources of protein and still have a fourfold margin of safety in pesticide intake compared to meat sources!

But parts per million take on practical significance only when we also consider the *amount* of food we eat in each food group. The same study reported that in the diet of a typical sixteen- to nineteen-year-old, meat, fish, and poultry contributed only 10 percent of the diet on a weight basis. (Note that this is an unusually low figure, much below the estimate given by the U.S. Department of Agriculture for the consumption pattern of the average adult.) But even at this *low* level of consumption, meat, fish, and poultry contributed *36 percent* of the total ingested chlorinated pesticides—or more than three times their proportion by weight in the diet.

In this study, the composition of the diet was such that the weight of dairy products, grains, cereals, potatoes, leafy vegetables, legumes, and root vegetables was about six times that of meat, fish, and poultry. Nevertheless, the total amount of pesticides contributed by dairy products *plus* these plant sources was less than that contributed by meat, fish, and poultry! I have included the complete statistics from this study in Appendix E for your convenience.

You may wish to note also that the types of dairy products considered in this study, which as a group showed the second highest level of pesticide contamination, were those with an average fat content of 8 to 13 percent. Since virtually all of the pesticide residues considered here (chlorinated hydrocarbons) are found in the fat, you could reduce your intake of pesticide residues by a judicious choice of low-fat dairy products like cottage cheese, low-fat milk, and yogurt.

In general, we have seen that plant foods contain less pesticide residues than foods of animal origin. It is probably fair to conclude that the principal explanation for this phenomenon is an ecological one: animals consuming large quantities of plant food accumulate biologically stable molecues like pesticides. But a key question still remains unanswered: aren't these patterns of pesticide contamination likely to change now that pesticides like DDT are being phased out? The answer is probably not to any great extent in the near future. Remember that the pesticide residues now in livestock are largely the result of *indirect* pesticide contamination coming from the general environment. As long as pesticides are in use on other agricultural products or in general use elsewhere, they seem to find their way into the body fat of higher organisms. Estimates of the life span of organochlorine pesticides already introduced into the environment range from seven to over forty years. In the case of extremely long food chains, recent calculations indicate that the maximum concentrations of pesticide residues derived from the *original* use of DDT in the 1940s may still not have been reached in the "highest" carnivores (e.g., eagles). Indeed, the pesticides currently in our ecosystem are not likely to reach equilibrium for another 100 to 200 years, *even if pesticide usage were to stop immediately!*[84]

You may also like to know whether or not the other potentially hazardous environmental contaminants you have been hearing about might actually be an unforeseen danger in eating vegetable foods. According to Dr. Lappé, the few reported studies on such things as mercury and arsenic show that these substances are present to about the same extent in foods of animal and vegetable origin. Grains and cereals come under close inspection because their seeds may be dressed with mercury to retard fungal growth and decay. However, in a study conducted in December 1967, meat, fish, and poultry were found to contain about the same amounts of mercury (0.036 ppm) as did grains and cereals (0.034 ppm).[35] It is perhaps noteworthy that dairy products and legumes had about a fifth of this amount.

Lest you be deceived by the seemingly modest levels of mercury contamination cited for fish above, note that this does not apply to *all* species. Some species are so heavily contaminated with heavy metals like mercury as to pose a real threat to human life. Almost all of the heavily contaminated fish discovered to date have been large oceanic species which are at the ends of long food chains. Even the game fish are contaminated with mercury in states like California where both agricultural and industrial effluents carry mercury into watersheds. Game fish like some species of trout in California and large oceanic fish like blue-fin tuna and swordfish may be contaminated with more than 0.5 milligram of mercury for every kilogram (2.2 pounds) of body weight. This concentration equivalent to 0.5 ppm is currently set as the "safety limit" for fish in this country. (Remember that this high limit assumes Americans eat very little fish.) Since only 70 milligrams of mercury are enough to kill you and mercury is one of those elements which can accumulate in the body, this is a real menace indeed —if you ate these species of fish in the same quantity that the average American eats meat, you could easily accumulate 10 to 20 milligrams of mercury in one year!

A fact not mentioned in the cited article is that tolerance limits in the U.S. for mercury through December 30, 1970, were set at *zero* because of its known toxic effects. Keeping mercury pollution down makes good health sense, but in a country that uses over 400 *tons* of costly mercury a year in its agriculture and industry, the Departments of Health, Education and Welfare and Agriculture *jointly* agreed that after December 31 zero tolerance would have to be dropped—such a level was considered "administratively impractical."[36]

But let's return to the more widespread problem of chlorinated pesticides where the potential health hazard is less clear. All of this discussion presupposes, of course, that you wish to reduce pesticide intake or that such reduction is desirable. Here is where there are likely to be differences of opinion. While everyone agrees that pesticide residues are an unfortunate concomitant to virtually all foods, experts seem to differ radically as to what constitutes a "health hazard." Thus, the authors of the article previously cited in the *Pesticide Monitoring Journal* felt obliged to point out that none of the levels of pesticide residues that they measured were likely to represent a health hazard. Indeed, less than 1 percent of the samples of foods in the meat, dairy, or fish category actually exceeded the then current toxicity standards established by the government.

A word to the wise: these toxicity standards are established on the basis of short-term toxicity tests on small animals. They say nothing about the possible *long-term* damage that pesticides may produce in humans such as chronic liver damage and possible cancer. There is evidence, for example, that DDT (as well as a number of currently less prevalent pestcides) produces cancer in mice when they are fed large amounts over protracted periods of time. Furthermore, the governmental agencies responsible for setting so-called "safety limits" or "tolerances" have proven themselves notoriously unreliable. Tolerance levels such as those set for the organophosphorous pesticides malathion and parathion were adjusted upward as the residue levels began to increase in milk samples in one state (Montana). Thus, "safety" will always be a matter of degree when it comes to biologically toxic pesticides and safety limits will continue to be adjusted to meet public outcry or agricultural exigency.

My purpose is to show you a way to minimize the amount of ecologically concentrated pesticide and heavy metal you ingest: by eating low on the food chain, you are simply reducing the quantity of most if not all pesticide residues in your diet. If we are wrong and there are no real health hazards that accrue from this period of environmental saturation with pesticides, then no harm has been done. If time shows that accumulated pesticide residues do produce damage to humans (and we may not know this for another ten or twenty years) then you may be grateful you heeded this cautionary note.

But even to have introduced the pesticide issue may seem to some of you a bit unfair. It may be an effective tactic in trying to convince the reader to eat less meat but does it relate directly to the theme of the book? A discussion of pesticides *is* particularly apposite here because our theme concerns the rational use of agricultural land.

In the last twenty years crop yields in the U.S. have increased sharply. The average annual yield of field corn, for example, jumped from 32.8 bushels per acre in the years 1941–45 to 50.1 bushels per acre in the years 1957–61 (an increase of 55 percent).[87] A major result of these greater yields, if not part of the impetus for them, has been to increase the amount of our agricultural yield available to livestock as feed. Currently, one-half of the yield of our harvested acreage is fed to animals, in part making possible our increase in meat consumption. (Beef and veal consumption has doubled in the U.S. in the last thirty-five years.)

Here is where pesticides enter in. These increased crop yields are almost entirely due to the introduction of the new kinds of pesticides in the mid-1940s. We might well ask whether it has been worth the cost of the subsequent contamination of our environment. We can observe the damage from pesticide residues to wildlife and speculate on their hazard to man. Like the waste of protein and like the overtaxing of our agricultural land, the presence of pesticide residues in our diet can be seen as yet another price we are paying for our unquestioning acceptance of increased meat production and consumption as an unassailable good. How often have I heard well-informed friends with concern about protecting the environment lament the fact that pesticides are a necessity. Organic agriculture would be ideal, they will say, but we couldn't feed 200 million people that way! I am not claiming to be able to estimate exactly how many people could be well-fed without the use of pesticides. *But*, the knowledge that we can presently afford to feed half of the yield of our harvested acreage to animals with so little return leads me to believe that we have an enormous "margin of safety" (or, more accurately, "margin of waste") in feeding our population. Curtailment of pesticide use might mean that we could no longer afford this extravagance and that our population would be eating less meat. But, as I hope the information in this book will make clear, eating well does not necessarily mean eating meat. But so far we've just been taking for granted that Americans eat an inordinate amount of meat. You would probably like to know

Rye

whether this is really true. So let's look at our protein consumption pattern.

I. Americans, the Protein "Heads"

Earlier I spoke of seeking a guideline for eating from the earth in a way that both maximizes the earth's potential to meet man's nutritional needs and at the same time minimizes the disruption of the earth necessary to sustain him. But all of the practices I've described are having just the opposite impact. Obviously my intent has been to suggest that we could reverse this pattern by consuming more plants directly, i.e., before they are put into the "protein factory in reverse"—livestock. But any suggestion for altering our protein-eating habits should be considered in the light of our current protein consumption patterns.

I recall reading a newspaper article reporting a survey in which Americans were asked: "What would be the first thing you would buy if you had extra income?" The majority answered, "Steak." Since meat consumption is associated with status in this country and is thought by many to be the key to good health, their answer is not at all surprising. The richer we get as a nation, the more meat, and hence, the more protein, we consume. The fact is that we are already consuming a greatly disproportionate amount of the world's supply of food from animals. Although North Americans comprise only 7 percent of the world population, we consume 30 percent of the world supplies of food of animal origin.[88]

In contrast to Asian Indians, for example, we eat about twice as much protein of all types; but we eat twelve times as much animal protein.[89] Obviously Asians get most of their protein from vegetable sources, while we get ours from meat. Indeed, whereas the Indian eats 2.85 pounds of meat and poultry in a year, an

American eats about 212 pounds, or seventy-five times as much.[40] And, the gap is widening. Since World War II the per capita protein available in the developing countries has *declined* by about 6 percent while that of the developed countries has increased by at least that much.[41]

No one would suggest that we should all be eating at the level of an average Indian. What is important, though, is whether or not Americans are *over*consumers, that is, to what extent we waste protein. How, you might ask, can a person waste the food he eats? If an individual isn't gaining weight or isn't actually overweight, doesn't he need all the food he eats? The answer is that although he may need the calories to maintain his weight, he may not necessarily need all the protein he is eating. The U.S. Department of Agriculture, undoubtedly not prone to overstatement, estimates that the average American eats from 10 to 12 percent *more* protein than his body can use as protein.[42] Since excess protein cannot be stored, it is converted to carbohydrate for use as an energy source. A very costly fuel!

And the trend of increased meat consumption is becoming more pronounced all the time. We are eating less grain and more meat than ever before: today we eat twice as much beef and veal[43] and two and a half times as much poultry[44] as we did about forty years ago.

The protein intake of the average American already exceeds the National Academy of Sciences' generous recommendation by 45 percent.[45, 46] And these statistics, based on the *availability* of protein, assume that each of us Americans is getting his fair share. Actually we know many people in the U.S. are protein-starved; this means that many others must be consuming several times the recommended allowance—an assumption borne out by statistics based on actual dietary interviews.

Now you've heard a lot about resource and protein waste—resulting from both America's livestock production practices and our excessive protein consumption. But what other choices are open to man? I have pointed to possible alternatives on an agricultural level, but what about on the level of our everyday diet? *Can* man rely more on plants and less on animals for protein? Just how suitable are plants for human protein nutrition? Since plant sources contribute 70 percent of the world's protein supplies,[47] it is a vital question indeed.

Part II

Bringing Protein
Theory Down to Earth

❧ ❧ ❧

Brazil nuts, Pistachios, Pine nuts

Having read of the enormous food resources man will willingly squander in the production of meat, you might easily conclude that meat—and meat in large quantities—must be indispensable to human well-being and endowed with qualities unmatched by other foods. This isn't the case, as I hope to demonstrate in this chapter. Hopefully this discussion will be useful to anyone wishing to rely more on plant protein and less on meat protein for *any* reason—be it ecological, ethical, financial, or medical.

Cashew nuts

A. Who Needs Protein Anyway?

Why can't people get by on a diet consisting solely of fats and carbohydrates? In the first place, while carbohydrates, fats, and protein all provide carbon, hydrogen, and oxygen, *only protein* contains nitrogen, sulfur, and phosphorus—substances which are essential to life. Even in purely quantitative terms protein's presence is quite impressive. We are 18 to 20 percent protein by weight! Just as cellulose provides the structural framework of a tree, protein provides the framework for animals. Skin, hair, nails, cartilage, tendons, muscles, and even the organic framework of bones are made up largely of fibrous proteins. Obviously, then, protein is needed for growth in children. But it is also needed by adults to replace tissues that are continually breaking down and to build tissues, like hair and nails, that continue growing.

Furthermore, the body depends on protein for the myriad reactions that we group under the heading "metabolism." As regulators of metabolic processes, we call certain proteins "hormones," and as catalysts of important metabolic reactions we call other proteins "enzymes." In addition, hemoglobin, the critical oxygen-carrying molecule of the blood, is a protein.

Not only is protein necessary to the basic chemical reactions of life, it is also necessary to maintain the body environment, so that these reactions can take place. Protein in the blood helps to prevent the accumulation of either too much base or too much acid. In this way it helps maintain "body neutrality," essential to normal cellular metabolism. Similarly, protein in blood serum participates in regulating the body's water balance—the distribution of fluids on either side of the cell membrane. (The distended stomachs of starving children are the result of protein deficiency, a state which allows fluid to accumulate in the interstitial spaces between the cells.)

Lastly, and of great importance, new protein synthesis is needed for antibody formation to fight bacterial and viral infections.

Not only do we need protein for all of these vital body processes but we need to renew our body's supply every day. Whereas it takes from a few days to seven years to deplete the body's reserves of other required nutrients, ammo acid reserves are depleted in a few hours.

So we need protein, but two basic questions still face us: how much and what kind? Since the answer to the question, "how much?," depends, in part, on "what kind?," I'll first explore the criteria by which we can distinguish among dietary proteins.

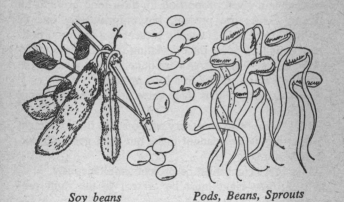

Soy beans   *Pods, Beans, Sprouts*

B. Quality Makes the Product

If all proteins were the same there would be no controversy about preferable protein sources for humans—

only quantity would matter. But proteins aren't identical. The proteins our bodies use are made up of twenty-two amino acids, in varying combinations. Eight of these amino acids can't be synthesized by our bodies; they must be obtained from outside sources. These eight essential amino acids (which I will refer to as EAAs) are *tryptophan, leucine, isoleucine, lysine, valine, threonine,* the *sulfur-containing amino acids,* and the *aromatic amino acids.*

To make matters more difficult, our bodies need each of the EAAs *simultaneously* in order to carry out protein synthesis. If one EAA is missing, even temporarily, protein synthesis will fall to a very low level or stop altogether.[48]

And to complicate things further, we need the EAAs in differing amounts. Basically, the body can use only *one* pattern of the EAAs. That is, each EAA must be present in a given proportion. In most food proteins all of the EAAs are present, but unfortunately one or more of the EAAs is usually present in a disproportionately small amount, thus deviating from the one utilizable pattern. These EAAs are quite rightfully called the "limiting amino acids" in a food protein.[49]

Let us put together these three critical factors about protein:

Of the twenty-two necessary amino acids, there are eight that our bodies cannot make but must get from outside sources.

All of these eight must be present simultaneously.

All of these eight must be present in the right proportions.

What does this mean to the body? A great deal. If you eat protein containing enough tryptophan to satisfy 100 percent of the utilizable pattern's requirement, 100 percent of the leucine level, and so forth, but only 50 percent of the necessary lysine, then, as far as your body is concerned, you might as well have eaten only 50 percent of *all* the EAAs. Only 50 percent of the protein you ate is used *as* protein and the rest is literally wasted. The protein "assembling center" in the cell uses the EAAs at the level of the "limiting amino acid" and releases the left-over amino acids to be used by the body as fuel as if they were lowly carbohydrates.[50] Chart III gives you a graphic illustration of what this means.

CHART III

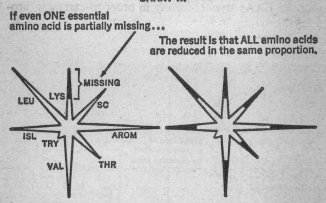

If even ONE essential amino acid is partially missing...

The result is that ALL amino acids are reduced in the same proportion.

MISSING

LEU LYS SC

ISL TRY AROM

VAL THR

This amount of protein in the food............Becomes... This amount of protein for your body to use.

One reflection of how closely the amino acid pattern of a given food matches that which the body can use is what nutritionists term the "biological value" of a food protein. Roughly, the "biological value" is the proportion of the protein absorbed by the digestive tract which is retained by the body. In other words, the biological value is the percentage of absorbed protein that your body actually uses. But there's another question: How much gets absorbed *to begin with* by the digestive tract?

That's what we call digestibility. So the protein available to our bodies depends on its biological value *and* its digestibility. The term covering both of these factors is *Net Protein Utilization* or NPU.[51] Quite simply, NPU tells us how much of the protein we eat is actually available to our body (see Chart IV).

CHART IV

WHAT IS "NPU"?

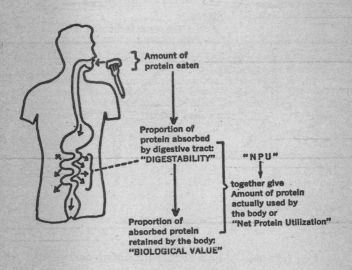

} Amount of protein eaten

Proportion of protein absorbed by digestive tract: "DIGESTABILITY"

"NPU"

together give Amount of protein actually used by the body or "Net Protein Utilization"

Proportion of absorbed protein retained by the body: "BIOLOGICAL VALUE"

NPU is a key concept used throughout the remainder of the book, so it is important to become completely comfortable with the term. Let's take another look at what determines the NPU of a given food protein. The NPU of a food is largely determined by how closely the essential amino acids in its protein match the body's one utilizable pattern. Because the protein of egg most nearly matches this ideal pattern, egg protein is used as

CHART V
Amino Acid pattern of EGG PROTEIN (solid lines)
as compared to patterns of:

PEANUT (dotted lines)

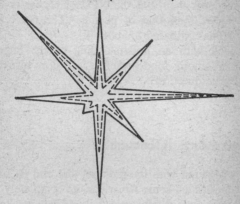

CHEESE (dotted lines)

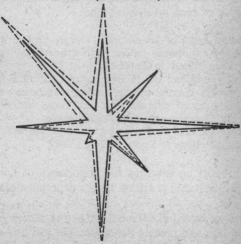

Source: *Amino Acid Content of Foods and Biological Data on Proteins,*
Food and Agricultural Organization of the U.N., Rome, 1970.

a model for measuring the amino acid patterns in other food. Let's take an example. A glance at Chart V will tell you that the amino acid pattern of cheese nearly matches egg's pattern while that of peanut fails utterly. You can guess then that the NPU of cheese is significantly higher than that of peanuts. The difference is great—70 as compared to about 40.

Prepared with an understanding of the important differences among food proteins, let's now turn to the second basic question:

C. How Much Is Enough?

Dissatisfaction with the national diet and its fixation on protein has led some Americans to completely reject the need for even a minimum daily protein intake. The *Berkeley Tribe* recently published an article reflecting the danger of such an overreaction:

> Several cases of *kwashiorkor* (severe protein malnutrition), a disease native to North Africa, (*sic*) have been found in Berkeley.
> An unpublished UC [University of California] hospital report blames certain fasting, vegetarian, and especially macrobiotic diets for this. Those diets often result in clinically protein-deficient people.
> Other ailments caused by protein-deficient diets are wound infections and poor healing ability.

This report underscores the importance of knowing the facts of protein nutrition before experimenting with a new diet.

So far we have talked about the two extremes—overconsumption and protein deficiency; but just how much protein is *enough*? We can arrive at a satisfactory answer. (Although, as you might expect, the experts disagree.) Determination of the proper protein allowance for a population involves three separate considerations: (1) minimum need; (2) an allowance for individual differences; and (3) an adjustment for protein quality. Fortunately, disagreement among nutritionists is limited to only the first consideration, the body's *minimum* need for protein. And even here the range of differences is small enough to make an average meaningful.

I. Minimum Need

Since nitrogen is a characteristic and relatively constant component of protein, scientists can measure protein by measuring nitrogen. To determine how much protein the body needs, experimenters first put subjects on a protein-free diet. They then measure how much nitrogen is lost in urine and feces. They add to this an amount to cover the small losses through the skin, sweat, and internal body structure. And, for children, additional nitrogen for growth is added. *The total of these nitrogen losses is the amount you have to replace by eating protein.* It is therefore the basis of the minimum protein requirement for body maintenance.

Since the major expert bodies on nutrition arrive at different conclusions using this "factorial" method, no established minimum now exists to guide us. Consequently, we must be satisfied with a base line which averages the values proposed by three major expert groups, the Food and Nutrition Board of the (U.S.) National Academy of Sciences,[52] the Canadian Board of Nutrition,[53] and the Food and Agriculture Organization of the U.N.[54] (I selected these particular groups because they are representative of the range of opinion among the many national bodies with protein standards.) The resulting recommended level of minimum intake is 0.214 grams per pound of body weight per day, which is close to the 0.227 gram level recommended by the National Academy of Sciences.

2. Allowance for Individual Differences

An allowance must also be made for individual differences. Fortunately most experts agree that a 30 percent allowance will cover 98 percent of a population.* Adding an allowance of 30 percent to our minimum requirement of 0.214 grams gives us an allowance of 0.278 grams, or *0.28 grams per pound of body weight per day.*

3. Adjustment for Protein Quality

Finally we must take into consideration the *kind* of protein eaten. Here is where we can apply our understanding of protein quality. Recall that the basic distinction among food proteins is how completely your body can use them. Because your body can't use low-quality protein as completely, it stands to reason that you must eat *more* of a low-quality protein than a high-quality protein to fill a daily protein allowance.

a. Allowance Based on Total Protein. But the protein allowance we've discussed so far holds only for the highest-quality protein, one that would be used *com-*

---

* The Food and Agriculture Organization differs slightly but with comparable results. They add 10 percent to the minimum requirement for losses due to stress and an allowance of 20 percent for individual differences.

pletely by the body. Since the total grams of protein eaten are *never* fully usable by the body, the task for nutritionists is to set appropriate protein allowances for different population groups, depending on the average usability of the protein (NPU) characteristic of that national diet. That is, the grams of *total* protein recommended must be increased to take into account the fact that not all the protein consumed can be used by the body. The formula for arriving at this allowance for grams of total protein is quite simple:

$$\text{Protein allowance if eating fully usable protein (0.28 grams per pound of body weight)} \times \frac{100}{\text{Net Protein Utilization characteristic of the national diet}} = \text{Grams of } \textbf{total} \text{ protein recommended for that population (per person/per pound body weight/per day)}$$

Using this formula it is easy to determine allowances for total protein suitable for different types of national diets—diets of high-quality protein needing fewer grams of total protein and diets of lower-quality protein needing more grams. For example, since 70 is the average value for protein quality (NPU) of a diet based largely on animal protein (meat, egg, milk), we insert 70 into our formula (0.28 gram X 100/70 = 0.40 gram). The result is an allowance of 0.40 gram of total protein per pound of body weight per day. For example, since the average American woman weighs 128 pounds (and consumes largely animal protein), her daily allowance is 51 grams of total protein, or 0.40 X 128 pounds. (If you have difficulty multiplying by 0.40, just double the weight, divide by five and you have the answer expressed in grams.)

Now we are on solid ground. And we are in a position to evaluate the allowance set for us as a population by the National Academy of Sciences. It is set at 0.42 gram per pound of body weight per day. At 0.42 gram it is 5 percent above the 0.40 gram which we have seen to be appropriate for a population getting most of its protein from animal sources. So now when a doctor tells you that you need 65 grams of protein a day, as an average male, or 54 grams, as an average female, you'll know where the figure comes from. The weight of the average American male and female (154 pounds and 128 pounds, respectively) is simply multiplied by 0.42 gram, the factor recommended by the National Academy of Sciences.

Consider now a diet based largely on plant protein. Since a typical value for the quality of plant protein is 55, a higher total protein allowance is called for. Inserting 55 into our formula, the result is 0.51 gram of total protein per pound of body weight per day (0.28 gram X 100/55 = 0.51 gram). Thus the recommended allowance for a 128-pound person in a population on a largely plant protein diet is 65 grams of total protein, or 0.51 X 128 pounds. (Notice that 0.51 is close to one-half; thus you can quickly estimate the grams of total protein needed for a person on a largely plant protein diet by dividing the body weight in half and expressing the answer in grams.)

b. *Allowance Based on Usable Protein.* But in this book where each food is listed individually, we can go one step further than generalizations about the protein quality in the diet of a whole population or an individual. In fact there is no need to generalize and to obscure the wide differences in protein quality of a mixed animal and plant protein diet. In such a diet only one-third of the protein from some sources is usable by your body while practically all the protein from other sources is usable. In the protein tables that make up Part III I have accounted for these differences by simply *adjusting the protein in each food to the level that is fully usable by the body*. Since *each food* is adjusted for protein quality, there is no need to apply the earlier formula based on an *average* level of protein quality. So, instead of talking about grams of total protein (only part of which the body can use), I'll be talking about grams of *usable* protein. Recall that the recommended daily protein allowance based on usable protein is 0.28 gram per pound of body weight, or 35.8 grams of usable protein a day for a person weighing 128 pounds and 43.1 grams for a person weighing 154 pounds.

This makes much more sense and will become even clearer to you in Part III where I explain how to use the protein food tables. But before reading on I'm sure you would like to have some idea of what the recommended intake of usable protein means in terms of the food you eat. Here are some comparisons, based on the

Sunflower and seeds

hypothetical assumption that you would be getting all of you day's protein from one source:

If you weigh:	To meet a day's allowance of usable protein:	YOU NEED					
		meat or fish	or milk	or eggs	or dry beans	or nuts
128 lb	35.8 g	7⅓ oz	8⅓ oz	5 cups	6	12¾ oz	12 oz
154 lb	43.1 g	9 oz	10 oz	6 cups	7	15⅓ oz	14½ oz

D. Protein Individuality

Before going on, a word of caution about putting too much stock in any figures purporting to deal with the "average" human being. R. J. Williams, a nutritionist who has devoted himself to the study of individual nutritional differences, illustrates dramatically the range of our "protein individuality." He points out that if beef were the only source of protein, one person's minimum protein needs could be met by two ounces of meat; yet another individual might require eight ounces.[55] Although over 98 percent of a population may not range more than 30 percent from an average requirement, these two possible extremes represent a *fourfold* difference in protein requirement! And, requirements for other nutrients are found to be equally, or even more widely, disparate.

Even more surprising perhaps is the fact that the need for protein can vary within the individual. Certain physical stress (pain, for example) or psychological stress (even from exam pressure) can cause one's protein requirement to jump by as much as one-third over ordinary needs.[56]

The obvious conclusion is this: *The fact that your friend is thriving beautifully on a low-protein diet tells you nothing about a diet suited to your own body's needs.* The best answer is to develop what Dr. Williams calls "body wisdom" which involves more than just being aware of how you feel—your energy level, general health, and temperament. Certain nutritional deficiencies have been shown to negatively affect one's appetite and choice of foods; so just feeling "satisfied" is not enough. Part of "body wisdom" involves being a wise observer of your body's condition. Because nails, hair, and skin require newly synthesized protein for growth and health, their condition is usually a good indication of whether or not you're getting enough protein. Similarily, notice whether or not abrasions heal quickly. If they don't, you may be seriously lacking protein in your diet.

Now that we can estimate the amount of protein that human beings must have (and understand how, in part, it depends on the type of protein eaten), we're ready to consider the really practical question: What are the best protein sources and how can we make best use of them? Since there is a great deal of "mythology" surrounding protein sources, let's first get our thinking straight about the useful distinctions to be made among them.

E. Is Meat Necessary?

Those who insist on the superiority, in fact indispensability, of meat as a protein source base their argument on both the large quantity and the high quality of protein in meat. Plant protein is seen as inferior on both counts. The result is that animal and vegetable protein are thought of as comprising two separate categories.

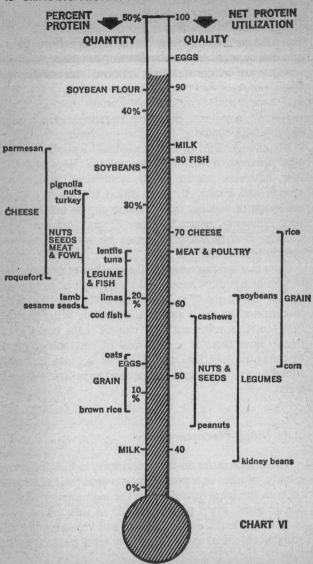

THE FOOD/PROTEIN CONTINUUM

In fact, this is a common mistake in our thinking about protein. For our nutritional concern here it is much more useful and accurate to visualize animal and vegetable protein as being on one continuum.

Chart VI, "The Food Protein Continuum," will help you see the range of protein variability on two scales: protein quantity, based on the percent of protein in the food by weight; and quality, based on the NPU or usability of the protein by the body.

Quantity: When judging protein with quantity as the criterion, generalization is difficult. However, it is clear that plants rank highest, particularly in their processed forms. Soybean flour is over 40 percent protein. Next comes certain cheeses such as Parmesan which is 36 percent protein. Meat follows, ranging between 20 and 30 percent. Dried beans, peas and lentils are essentially in the same category, that is, between 20 and 25 percent protein. At the bottom end of the quantity scale we find examples of both animal and plant protein. We find grains here and, though it might surprise you, milk and eggs also. There are, of course, other plants, some fruit, for example, that contain too little protein to even appear on the scale. (We're concerned here only with plants that are widely used as sources of protein.)

Quality: The protein quality scale generally ranges from NPU values of about 40* to 94. Clearly animal protein occupies the highest rungs of this scale. Meat, however, is not at the top. It places slightly above the middle with an average NPU of 67. At the top are egg (NPU of 94) and milk (NPU of 82). The NPUs of plant proteins generally range lower on the continuum, between 40 and 70. However, protein in some plants such as soybeans and whole rice approach or overlap the NPU values for meat. But the general distribution

----

* Most of the NPU values used throughout the book are taken from a United Nations publication.[57]

of animal protein high on the NPU scale and plant protein lower on this scale tells us that the proportions of essential amino acids found in most animal protein more nearly match human body requirements than the proportions commonly found in plants. This means that in general you need to eat proportionately less meat protein than plant protein to be "covered" for the essential amino acid requirements.

But people don't have to depend on meat for protein and the correct supply of amino acids. There are several other alternatives:

1) Eat large amounts of "lower-quality" plant protein, enough so that you will get an adequate amount of even the "limiting amino acids."
2) Eat alternate animal protein sources such as dairy products.
3) Eat a variety of plant proteins which have mutually complementary amino acid patterns.

When eating plant protein from a single plant source (such as beans or rice) you're likely to be limited in the amount of protein your body can utilize because of a limiting amino acid (for beans the limiting amino acids are the sulfur-containing amino acids and for rice they are isoleucine and lysine). Consequently, a major drawback of the first alternative is that you would have to eat (and *waste!*) relatively enormous quantities of your protein source in order to insure your daily protein requirement.

The advantage of the second choice is that diary products have high-quality protein, in fact better values for protein utilization (NPU) than meat. But by itself, of course, this alternative is gastronomically dull; and moreover, since protein conversion even by dairy cattle entails some waste of protein, why rely on this alternative more than you have to?

The third alternative means eating, in the *same meal,*

different plant foods in which the amino acid deficiency of one item is supplemented by the amino acid contained in others. (Remember that the EAAs must be present simultaneously.) It is more efficient than the first alternative because the complementary effect of the mixture means that more of the protein *can be used* by the body (less is lost and converted to fuel). And it is more efficient than the second choice because it takes optimal advantage of more abundant plant protein.

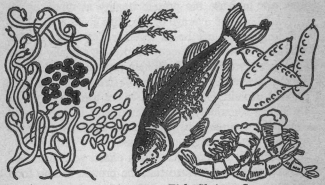

Mung bean sprouts, Rice, Fish, Shrimp, Snow peas

F. Complementing Your Proteins

Obviously the best solution is to use both the second and third alternatives. This means combining different plant sources, or nonmeat animal protein sources with plant sources, in the *same* meal. Most people do this to some extent anyway, just as a matter of course. Eating a mixture of protein sources can increase the protein value of the meal; here's a case where *the whole is greater than the sum of its parts*. To repeat, this is true because the EAA deficiency in one food can be met by the EAA contained in another food. For example, the expected biological value of three parts white bread and one part cheddar cheese would be 64 if there were no supplementary relationship. Yet, if eaten together, the actual biological value is 76! [58] The "whole" is greater largely because cheese fills bread's lysine and isoleucine deficiencies. Such protein mixes *do not result in a perfect protein* that is fully utilizable by the body (remember that only egg is near perfect). But combinations can increase the protein quality as much as 50 percent above the average of the items eaten separately.

Eating wheat and beans together, for example, can increase by about 33 percent the protein actually usable by your body. Chart VII will help you see why. It shows the four essential amino acids most likely to be deficient in plant protein. On each side, where beans and wheat are shown separately, we see large gaps in amino acid content as compared to egg protein. But, if we put the two together, these gaps are closed.

To exploit this complementary effect, you can make dishes and plan meals so that the protein in one food

Spinach, Onion, Garlic, Sesame

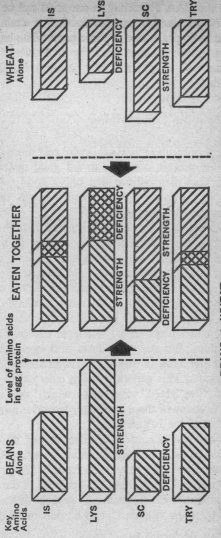

CHART VII

DEMONSTRATING PROTEIN COMPLEMENTARITY

Key Amino Acids

BEANS Alone

Level of amino acids in egg protein

EATEN TOGETHER

WHEAT Alone

IS

LYS — STRENGTH

SC — DEFICIENCY

TRY

STRENGTH

DEFICIENCY

STRENGTH

DEFICIENCY

DEFICIENCY

STRENGTH

BEANS + WHEAT =
COMPLEMENTARY PROTEIN COMBINATION

Source: *Amino Acid Content of Foods and Biological Data on Proteins,*
Food and Agricultural Organization of the U.N., Rome, 1970.

fills the amino acid deficiencies in another food. A bit laborious, you say? It's not as hard as it sounds! And to prove it, I've included many recipes* to guide (and tempt) you. But the real fun for you might be "inventing" your own complementary protein combinations.

G. Protein Isn't Everything

Many people who might otherwise rely more on plant sources for protein continue to eat great quantities of meat because they believe that only "good red meat" can supply the many vitamins and minerals that their bodies needs. Are they right?

A national food survey in Britain in 1966[59] showed that, although 40 percent of the protein in a typical British diet comes from plant sources, *plants provide, on the average, more than twice the amount of vitamins and minerals provided by meat and fish.* Seven nutrients were considered: vitamin A, thiamine, riboflavin, niacin, vitamin C, calcium, and iron. Plant sources were the greatest contributors of all nutrients except riboflavin and calcium. But dairy products and eggs, *not meat,* provided the bulk of the daily requirements of these two nutrients. This general pattern emerged in spite of the fact that green vegetables, which are valuable sources of many of these nutrients, comprise a relatively minor part of the British diet.

A breakdown of sources of vitamins and minerals in the American diet reveals a similar pattern. Although plant sources provide only 31 percent of the protein in our national diet, they provide 50 percent of the vitamin A, 59 percent of the thiamine, 53 percent of the niacin, 94 percent of the vitamin C, and 62 percent of the iron.

---

* See Part IV, Section B.

As in the British study, dairy products contribute the largest percentage of both riboflavin and calcium.[60]

Other important nutrients not covered by the British survey include phosphorus, potassium, and magnesium. Although meat is a good source for both phosphorus and potassium, there are nonmeat sources which are even better. Whereas meat and fish contain 250 to 274 milligrams (mg) of phosphorus per 100 grams (3½ ounces), cheddar cheese contains 478 mg and peanuts 401 mg. Meat contains from 290 to 390 mg of potassium per 100 grams, but a baked potato has 503 mg and lima beans 422 mg. In the case of magnesium, meat is actually among the poorer sources. Rich sources include cocoa, nuts, soybeans, whole grains, and green leafy vegetables.[61]

In fact, the only required nutrient thought to be limited strictly to animal sources is cobalamin (vitamin B_{12}).[62] But there are potentially significant exceptions to this rule. A type of blue-green algae, *Spirulina maxima* (a popular food in parts of Africa), and two other algae all contain cobalamin.[63] Thus, it is possible, at least theoretically, to fill all man's nutritional needs from plant sources. For most of you, however, the important fact is that there is no danger of cobalamin deficiency as long as you eat dairy products or eggs.

Thus, we can safely conclude that a varied plant protein diet supplemented with dairy products and eggs can supply sufficient protein while at the same time surpassing meat in the provision of some of the other basic nutrients. All this is not meant to belittle the nutritional value of meat. My aim is only to provide a more realistic view of the wide variety of nutritious foods sources to replace the culturally fixed idea of the absolute supremacy of meat.

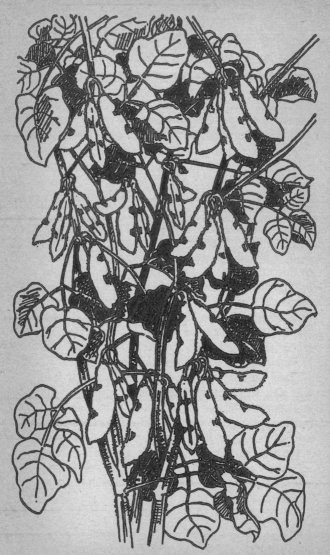

Soy beans

Part III

Eating from the Earth: Protein Theory Applied

ℐ ℐ ℐ

A. Protein Without Meat: A Daily Guide

Now that you understand the necessity of adequate protein intake and the importance of protein quality, this section will combine both concepts in a series of tables that you can apply to your daily eating habits. Here foods are grouped into major categories, evaluated as to their protein merit, and ranked according to their contribution to your daily protein requirement. But first the rationale for selecting the particular foods included in the charts.

1. The Calorie Criterion

Since most foods contain *some* protein, if you could consume an unlimited quantity of food every day, you would eventually fill your protein need! But, if you wish to get enough protein without putting on weight, a calorie guideline is necessary to define a good protein source.

My guideline is based on this formula: A young man of 154 pounds should consume about 2800 calories a day and 43.1 grams of usable protein*; or 65 calories

---

* If you'd like to review the meaning of "usable" protein, turn back to Part II, Sections B and C.

for each gram of protein. A young woman of 128 pounds should consume about 2000 calories a day and 43.1 grams of usable protein; or 56 calories for each gram. Therefore, in order not to gain weight and still get enough protein, the calorie/protein ratio shouldn't exceed these limits; that is, an average ratio of about 60:1. In fact, some of your protein sources should be well below this ratio to make room in your diet for items like fruit, which provide calories and vitamins but essentially no protein.

With few exceptions, the foods in the following protein tables observe the 60:1 ratio of calories to protein. Potato chips, for example, are 5 percent protein; but they were excluded because they have a ratio of about 179 calories per gram of usable protein. Similarly, English walnuts (about 88:1) and pecans (about 149:1) aren't listed.

2. Unprocessed Criterion

Only unprocessed or "less-processed" foods (such as whole wheat flour as opposed to white flour) are in-

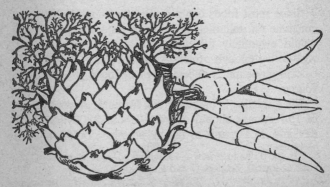

Artichoke, Carrots

cluded because they are generally higher in protein and other nutrients. (See the Appendices F, G, and H for comparisons of brown with white rice, whole wheat flour with white flour, and a variety of sugar sources.)

3. Protein Content Criterion

Finally, even though many more vegetables probably meet the caloric criterion, they were excluded if an *average* serving provides less than two grams of total protein.

B. How To Use the Tables

The first two columns in the protein tables tell you what percent of your daily protein need is met by an average serving of a given food. The items are ranked in *decreasing* order according to the percent of their contribution to your daily protein requirement, both within each food category and by food category.* *To fulfill your protein allowance these percentages must add up to 100 percent each day.*

These percentages reflect the recommended protein allowance of 0.28 gram of *usable* protein per pound of body weight. (Recall that this allowance includes a 30 percent increase above the minimum requirements to take individual differences into account.) The last three columns of the tables show you the basis on which I arrived at these percentages: The *total* grams of protein

---

* Except for meat and poultry, placed last, because they are primarily included for the sake of comparison with nonmeat protein sources.

have been reduced by the NPU score* of the food to arrive at the grams of protein *your body can use*. This amount of usable protein I then divided by the daily protein allowance to get the percent of the daily protein allowance that an average serving fills. Simple enough.

To remind you of the importance of adjusting for protein usability, let me give you a graphic example. If, for instance, we considered that eating one-half ounce of egg protein was the same as eating one-half ounce of peanut protein we would be greatly mistaken. The amino acid pattern of the egg protein (NPU of 94) is one that the body can use completely; but, the body can only use half of the peanut protein (NPU of 43) because its amino acids deviate considerably from the body's one utilizable pattern. So if you eat one-half ounce each of egg and peanut protein you get twice as much protein from the egg as from the peanut. The percentages shown in the charts have been calculated to correct for these differences in the availability of protein to your body.

The only difficulty in adjusting for differences in protein usability is that research to determine the NPU scores of food proteins is still rudimentary. Many plant foods have not been tested and the NPU scores that we do "know" are often based on a limited number of experiments. We can hope that this research will progress. In the meantime, even with rough estimates of protein quality, we are on better ground than if our calculations were based on *total* protein knowing full well that 5 to 70 percent of this total is not usable by the body.

The percentages in the first two columns apply to the average American adult—a 154-pound male and a 128-pound female. If you are not quite so average, use this

---

* In addition to the 1970 U.N. publication on protein already cited,[57] other sources were used in estimating NPUs.[64-67]

guideline for determining the appropriate protein intake for your body weight:

Female		Male	
If your weight is:	The percentages should add up to:	If your weight is:	The percentages should add up to:
108 lb	85	154 lb	100
118	90	164	105
128	100	174	115
138	110	184	120
148	115	194	125

Add up your protein intake for a few days to see whether or not you are meeting your protein allowance. If not, use the tables to figure out ways to increase your intake and let it become a habit!

Let me emphasize that these values are for the "average adult." Pregnant women in the second and third trimester are advised to increase their protein intake by 35 percent and lactating women by 70 percent.* Children also need one and a half to two times more protein per pound of body weight than adults; and babies from two to three times more.

Mixing Your Own Proteins. Next to the percentages in the tables are letter ratings which allow you to make up your own complementary protein combinations. The letter ratings indicate how well each type of food supplies you with a key amino acid. (Of the eight essential amino acids, only the four likely to be deficient in a diet of nonmeat protein are shown here.) Since egg protein is considered to be the most nearly perfect protein, the ratings are based on how closely the particular amino acid content of a food matches the amount of that amino acid found in egg protein.† Thus:

* Women on low-protein diets abort about twice as often in early pregnancy as women on high-protein diets.

† The amino acid content of egg protein used by scientists as the model is that established by the U.N. Expert Group, reported in *Protein Requirements* (WHO, FAO), 1965.

Letter Ratings: Percent of Egg Amino Acid Content

A+ $>$ 100	C = 40–60
A = 80–100	D = 20–40
B = 60–80	E = 1–20

Using these tables you can match the deficiencies in some foods (C and D ratings) with adequacies (A and B ratings) in other foods in order to achieve higher biological values than those of the same foods eaten separately. Discovering the patterns of amino acid strengths and weaknesses in the different food groups will enable you to do your own "protein matching." To help you I have provided two guides:

(1) For foods having no serious amino acid deficiencies such as seafood (Table I) page 68, dairy products (Table II) page 74, and meat and poultry (Table VIII) page 99. I have emphasized their particular strengths by putting their A+ ratings in boldface. These foods need no supplementation from other foods but make excellent supplements themselves.

(2) All the other tables have foods with serious amino acid deficiencies. The one or two most important weaknesses of each food are indicated by boxed letters. Compensation for these deficiencies can come either from the foods in category (1) above or from other foods having an *opposite* pattern of amino acid deficiency. Rather than concentrating on the names of amino acids, it might be easier simply to note the columns in which weaknesses tend to occur. The following examples will help you see how easy it is.

Let's say you wanted to serve split pea soup for supper. What would you choose to go with it? You can see with a glance at Table III (page 78) that, like other legumes, the amino acid weaknesses of peas occur in the two *outside* columns. Obviously you would want to avoid serving another food with the same weaknesses. You would look for a food with just the opposite pattern, one with boxed letters in the two *inside* columns. Such a food has assets that could meet peas' deficits and vice versa. Leafing through the tables, you will discover several choices. Look at Table IV (page 81). Sesame seed is an excellent match. Why not sesame-honey cookies for dessert, or, for the last-minute cook, toasted sesame meal on or in the soup? Walnuts might also be a good match. Would you enjoy a Waldorf salad chock full of walnuts? Perhaps a more obvious match for your pea soup is found in Table V (page 88), the grains. You might choose, for example, a rice side dish. Or you may even wish to combine both possibilities for supplementing the soup, that is, a seed-grain combination such as whole wheat–sesame muffins. Simpler yet would be to spread sesame butter on bread to eat with your soup. (You'll find instructions for making sesame butter among the Basic Cooking Instructions, Appendix A.)

But what if you are having potato salad for lunch? Notice in Table VI (page 92), that potatoes, like many other fresh vegetables, are deficient in the amino acids of the *second* and *last* columns. Because this pattern is not so easily matched you might wish to seek a solution in the dairy family (Table II, page 74), a food group having no serious deficiencies. Try the cheeses. In the second and last columns they have B and A ratings which can compensate for the D and C deficiencies of potato. Your lunch, then, can easily become protein-sound: a plate of potato salad and cottage cheese (with chives in the cottage cheese and tomato on the side, if you like). But don't overlook the most obvious way of "fixing" potatoes: let egg compensate for potatoes' weaknesses. Try adding plenty of hard-boiled egg to the salad.

Researchers point out, however, that the technique of combining proteins based on amino acid patterns is

Seafood

limited because the availability to the body of the stated amounts of amino acid varies.[68] Acknowledging this limitation, I've emphasized the amino acid ratings on the assumption that you will have more utilizable protein in your diet by combining foods on the basis of their amino acid patterns than if selection were random. My assumption seems valid because most of the combinations experimentally shown to have a mutually complementary effect could be deduced from the deficiencies which show up in their ratings here. Following these tables you find many recipes based on protein combinations which have been shown experimentally to have a complementary relationship.

Protein Tables

1. Seafood

Seafood rates first place as a source of protein. Fish is near meat in protein content and superior to meat in protein quality (NPU), except for shark and skate. Some fish like cod and haddock (#13 and #15 on Table I) are practically *pure* protein. That is, they contain *no* carbohydrates and only about 0.1 percent fat. Though the average protein portion I have given is small (less than ¼ pound), even at this level some fish can fill 40 to 50 percent of your daily allowance. It doesn't take much: even small chunks of fish in soups and lightly cooked vegetable mixes can give the dish a taste and protein boost.

The next to the last column of the table tells you about the protein quality of seafood: the high NPU of most fish, 80, reflects excellent amino acid ratings. Notice particularly the high lysine content (A+ rating) of seafood. It is now easy to explain why fish and rice is successfully eaten as a staple by so many people. Rice, as

Table I. SEAFOOD

Average Servings of 3½ oz (100 g) in Decreasing Order of Usable Protein	Percent of Daily Protein Allowance in an Average Serving		Ratings of Amino Acid Content as Compared to Egg Protein				Total Grams of Protein	NPU	Grams of Protein your Body Can Use[2]
	M	F	Tryp.	Iso.	Lys.	S.-C.[1]			
					STRENGTH →				
1. Tuna,† canned in oil, drained, ⅞ cup	44%	53%	B	B	A+	B	24	(80)	19
2. Mackerel, Pacific	41	50	B	B	A+	B	22	(80)	18
3. Halibut	39	47	B	B	A+	C	21	(80)	17
4. Humpback salmon	37	45	B	B	A+	B[3]	20	(80)	16
5. Swordfish[3]	35	42	B	B	A+	B	19	(80)	15
6. Striped bass	35	42	B	B	A+	B[3]	19	(80)	15
7. Rockfish	35	42	B	B	A+	B	19	(80)	15
8. Shad	35	42	B	A	A+	B	19	(80)	15
9. Shrimp	35	42	B	B	A+	B[4]	19	*(~80)	15
10. Sardines, Atlantic, 8 med., canned in oil	32	39	B	A	A+	B	21	69	14
11. Carp	32	39	B	B	A+	A[3]	18	(80)	14
12. Catfish	32	39	B	B	A+	A	18	(80)	14

†Warning: Large ocean-going fish like blue-fin tuna and swordfish which are at the end of long food chains have been shown to be heavily contaminated with mercury. See page 25 for exact data.

Average Servings of 3½ oz (100 g) in Decreasing Order of Usable Protein	Percent of Daily Protein Allowance in an Average Serving		Ratings of Amino Acid Content as Compared to Egg Protein				Total Grams of Protein	NPU	Grams of Protein your Body Can Use[2]
	M	F	Tryp.	Iso.	Lys.	S.-C.[1]			
					STRENGTH				
					→				
13. Cod	32%	39%	B	B	A+	A	18	(80)	14
14. Pacific herring	32	39	B	A	A+	B	18	(80)	14
15. Haddock	32	39	B	B	A+	A	18	(80)	14
16. Crab	32	39	B	B	A+	B[4]	17	*(~80)	14
17. Northern lobster	32	39	B	B	A+	B[4]	17	*(~80)	14
18. Squid	30	36	A	B	A+	B	16	*(~80)	13
19. Scallops, 2 or 3	28	34	B	B	A+	B	15	*(~80)	12
20. Flounder or sole	28	34	A	B	A+	C	15	(80)	12
21. Clams, 4 large, 9 small	26	31	B	B	A+	B	14	*(~80)	11
22. Oysters, 2 to 4	21	25	A	B	A+	B	11	*(~80)	9

[1]Amino Acids: Tryp. = Tryptophan; Lys. = Lysine; Iso. = Isoleucine; S.-C. = Sulphur-containing amino acids.
These are the four essential amino acids likely to be deficient in plant protein.
[2]Loss calculated from the Net Protein Utilization score (NPU). See page 000 for an explanation of NPU.
[3]Also slightly deficient in the aromatic amino acids, phenylalanine and tyrosine.
[4]Also slightly deficient in valine.
*~ = estimated

you will see, is deficient in lysine and isoleucine—defects which seafood can effectively remedy.

I have given the values for raw as opposed to cooked seafood only because the best data available to me was in this form. No significant amount of protein is lost in cooking seafood.

Tips for complementing other foods with seafood

The lysine strength (A+) of seafood means that it can complement well the protein of foods low in lysine such as grains and certain nuts and seeds.

---

2. Dairy Products

In Part II you may have been surprised to discover that dairy products appear low on the quantity scale of the "Food Protein Continuum." It's true that their percent protein on a weight basis is low. However, the fact that milk (#5 in Table II, page 74) is only 4 percent protein and eggs (#9) are only 13 percent protein should not mislead you. Remember that the quality of these products is higher than any other food. On the right side of Table II, placed over the arrows, you can read their NPU scores—the measures of protein quality. The NPU of milk is over 80 and that of egg is 94 as compared to beef, for example, with an NPU of 67.

An example will remind you of the importance of NPU. Although eggs *appear* to have much *less* protein than beans (that is, eggs are only 13 percent protein while beans are 21 percent protein), as far as your body is concerned their protein content is nearly equal. Why? Because the high NPU of eggs means that its protein

Cheeses

is almost fully used by the body while the low NPU of beans makes its protein only partly available.

Also, the relatively low protein content of some dairy products is made up for by the fact that they are in forms which we normally eat in large quantities. For example, two cups of milk (#5 on Table II) supplies more than one-third of your daily protein allowance. Let's compare this with another food, noodles (#3 on Table V), whose protein content is *three times* that of milk. To get the same proportions of your daily protein allowance from noodles as from two cups of milk, you would have to eat *four cups* of cooked noodles. The point is that whereas you might easily drink two cups of milk a day, you are not likely to eat four cups of noodles!

You will discover in the protein cost and calorie comparisons following the tables (Charts VIII and IX) that dairy products fare quite well on these counts also. And dairy products have another "virtue" to recommend them. They are our major source of calcium. This nutritional strength takes on special importance in light of the fact that the majority of American women consume

Tips for using dairy products to complement the protein in other foods

1. **Amino Acid Makeup:** Dairy products have excellent amino acid ratings as you would suppose from their high NPU scores. Thus, they make good supplements to any food. But dairy products have notable amino acid strengths in isoleucine, and, especially, in lysine. These strengths can be used to advantage in combination with cereal grains (Table V)—low in both of these same amino acids. And, it doesn't take much! Only two tablespoons of nonfat dried milk added to one cup of wheat or rye flour increases the protein quality about 45 percent. Thus, bread with cheese, cheese-rice casseroles, and cereal with milk are all good protein mixes. These same amino acid strengths allow dairy products to complement the protein of nuts and seeds (Table IV, sesame, peanuts, black walnuts, etc.).

2. Experimentally determined complementary protein mixes include milk products: **For recipes see pages:**

plus Grains, for example:

Milk + Rice	162–68
Milk + Wheat	169–75
Milk + Corn + Soy	202–8
Milk + Wheat + Peanuts	239–47

plus Nuts and seeds, for example:

Milk + Peanuts	
Milk + Sesame	248–52

plus Legumes, for example:

Milk + Beans	209–14

plus Potatoes:

Milk + Potatoes	253–57

considerably less than the recommended allowance of calcium. But some people hesitate to increase their intake of dairy products because of their fat content. This shouldn't be a stumbling block—not when there are so many delicious ways to enjoy low-fat dairy products. Try some of the suggestions in the special section on low-fat dairy products, Section E.

3. Legumes (Dried Peas, Beans, and Lentils)

Legumes are one of the earliest crops cultivated by man. Even in Biblical times their nutritional value was known. When Daniel and other favored children of Israel were offered the meat usually reserved only for the King of Babylon, Daniel refused. He asked only for pulses (legumes) and water. After ten days, the Bible passage relates, the faces of the children "appeared fairer and fatter than all the children that ate of the king's meat." This is not too surprising because the protein content of some legumes is actually equal to, or greater than, that of meat! But maybe you are registering surprise that anyone would *choose* legumes. It is true that dried peas and beans can be the dullest food in the world. But they can also be the basis of the most savory dishes in your menu. Lentils, peas, black beans, and soybeans make delicious and satisfying soups. (See *The Natural Foods Cookbook,* pp. 68–70.) Kidney beans and garbanzos (chickpeas) make a great cold salad or they can top off a fresh green salad. Peabeans with maple syrup is the old favorite—Boston baked beans.

Since legumes are all at least 20 percent protein, why don't they contribute even more to meeting our daily protein allowance than the typical 10 to 20 percent indicated on the table? The answer is twofold: Their

Table II. DAIRY PRODUCTS

Average Serving of Dairy Products	Percent of Daily Protein Allowance in an Average Serving		Ratings of Amino Acid Content as Compared to Egg Protein				Total Grams of Protein	NPU	Grams of Protein your Body Can Use
	M	F	Tryp.	Iso.	Lys.	S.-C.			
					STRENGTH →				
1. Cottage cheese, 6 tbsp, 3½ oz (100 g)									
Uncreamed	30	36	B	A	A+	B	17	(~75)	13
Creamed	26	31	B	A	A+	B	14		11
2. Egg white, dried, powdered, ½ oz (14 g)	21	25	A+	B	A+	A+	11	(83)	9
3. Milk, nonfat dry solids, 1 oz (5½ tbsp inst.)	19	22	A	B	A+	B	10	(82)	8
4. Parmesan cheese, 1 inch sq, 1 oz (28 g)	16	20	B	A	A+	B	10	(~70)	7
5. Milk, skim, whole or buttermilk, 1 c (244 g)	16	20	A	A	A+	B	9	(82)	7
6. Yogurt from skim milk, 1 c (244 g)	16	20	A	A	A+	B	8	(82)	7
7. Swiss cheese, 1 inch sq, 1 oz (28 g)	14	17	B	A	A+	B	8	(~70)	6

Average Serving of Dairy Products	Percent of Daily Protein Allowance in an Average Serving		Ratings of Amino Acid Content as Compared to Egg Protein				Total Grams of Protein	NPU	Grams of Protein your Body Can Use
	M	F	Tryp.	Iso.	Lys.	S.-C.			
					STRENGTH →				
8. Edam cheese, 1 inch sq, 1 oz (28 g)	14	17	B	A	A+	B	8	(~70)	6
9. Egg, 1 medium (48 g)	14	17	A	A	A+	A	6	(94)	6
10. Ricotta cheese, ¼ cup (60 g)	12	14	B	A	A+	B	7	(~75)	5
11. Cheddar cheese, 1 in sq, 1 oz (28 g)	12	14	B	A	A+	B	7	(70)	5
12. Roquefort cheese, or Blue mold, 1 in sq, 1 oz (28 g)	9	11	B	A	A+	B	6	(~70)	4
13. Camembert cheese, 1 inch sq, 1 oz (28 g)	9	11	B	A	A+	B	5	(~70)	4
14. Ice cream, about 1/5 pint (100 g)	9	11	A	A	A+	B	5	(~82)	4

The following dairy products are not good protein sources because they contain too many calories for the amount of protein you get[1]: cream   sour cream   cream cheese   butter (no protein).

[1] See page 105 for an explanation of the selection of good protein sources based on their calorie to protein ratio.

NPU scores are on the average lower than any other food group recommended as a protein source. Lentils (#11) have the lowest NPU score, 30, of any food included in these tables. But legumes also include some of the highest-quality plant protein. Soybeans and mung beans (#1 and #2) have NPU scores of 61 and 57, respectively—reflecting protein quality approaching that of meat. (Note that soybean curd, *tofu,* has an even higher NPU, 65, than the untreated soybean.) Secondly, we tend to eat legumes in small quantities. A serving of three-fourths cup of legumes actually weighs only 50 grams before cooking. We usually eat other high-protein food like meat in quantities at least twice this amount. But remember the percentages I have given you here are for legumes eaten *without* the benefit of supplementation with other protein sources. Eating legumes with cereals can make the protein *in both* more valuable to you—increasing the availability of their combined protein content as much as 40 percent. On the basis of their amino acid letter ratings, let us see how this is possible.

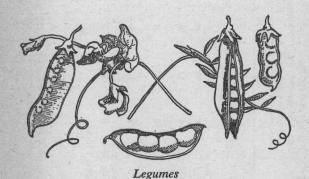

Legumes

Tips for complementing the protein in legumes

1. **Amino Acid Makeup:** Notice in Table III (page 78), that the major amino acid deficiencies of legumes appear in the two **outside** columns, tryptophan and the sulfur-containing amino acids. But, among the nuts and seeds in Table IV (page 81), and among the grains in Table V (page 88), deficiencies appear most frequently in the two **inside** columns, isoleucine and lysine. It is now clear why legume protein, on the one hand, and the protein in grains and certain nuts and seeds, on the other hand, complement each other. Having exactly the opposite strengths and weaknesses, in combination they become more complete proteins.

2. Experimentally determined complementary protein mixes include legumes:

	For recipes see pages:
plus Grains, for example:	
Legumes + Rice	133–39
Soybeans + Rice + Wheat	146–50
Beans + Wheat	176–80
Soybeans + Corn + Milk	202–8
Beans + Corn	195–201
Soybeans + Wheat + Sesame	189–94
plus Milk products, for example:	
Beans + Milk	209–14
plus Nuts and seeds, for example:	
Soybeans + Peanuts + Sesame	227–32
Soybeans + Peanuts + Wheat + Rice	220–26
Soybeans + Sesame + Wheat	189–94

Table III. LEGUMES (Dried Beans, Peas, Lentils)

Average Serving of Legumes, ¼-⅓ c dry[1] (Approx. 50 g)	Percent of Daily Protein Allowance in an Average Serving		Ratings of Amino Acid Content as Compared to Egg Protein				Total Grams of Protein	NPU	Grams of Protein Your Body Can Use
	M	F	Tryp.	Iso.	Lys.	S.-C.			
If complemented add 5%			DEFICIENCY			DEFICIENCY			
1. Soybeans or soy grits	23	28	A	B	A+	C[2]	17	(61)	10
2. Mung beans	16	20	C	B	A+	D	12	(57)	7
3. Broad beans	14	17	C	B	A+	D	13	(48)	6
4. Peas	14	17	C	B	A	D	12	(47)	6
5. Black beans	12	14	B	A+	A+	D	12	(42)	5
6. Cowpeas (blackeye)	12	14	B	C	A+	C	12	(45)	5
7. Kidney beans	12	14	C	B	A+	D	11	(38)	5
8. Chickpeas (garbanzos)	12	14	C	B	A+	D	10	(43)	5
9. Lima beans	12	14	C	B	A+	C		(52)	5
10. Tofu (soybean curd), wet weight, 3½ oz, 2"x2"x2½"	12	14	A		A	D	8	(65)	5
11. Lentils	9	11	C	B	A+	C D	13	(30)	4
12. Other common beans, navy, peabean, white	9	11	C	B	A+	D[2]	11	(38)	4

[1]Makes ¾ to 1 c when cooked.
[2]Also deficient in valine.
See pages 64-65 for explanation of boxed letters.

Nuts and Seeds

4. Nuts and Seeds

Nuts and seeds follow legumes in their ability to meet your daily protein need. They rank behind legumes only because we tend to eat them in much smaller quantities and they therefore contribute less to our dietary needs. Actually they are as rich in protein as the legumes, and they often have higher NPU values.

First let's compare the two seeds, sesame and sunflower. Sunflower seed is definitely richer in protein than is sesame—19 percent as compared to 24 percent. The quality of sunflower protein is also better than sesame protein—probably the result of the lower lysine and isoleucine content of sesame seed. Experimentally, sunflower seeds show even greater ability to promote growth than meat. But both types of seed have higher NPU scores than most legumes.

You might also wish to note that sesame seeds lose most of their calcium, iron, thiamine, and all of their sodium, potassium, and Vitamin A when they are decorticated. To avoid this loss you can purchase the "unhulled" variety.

Now look at the nuts. The quantity and quality of their protein is generally lower than the seed meals. A surprise is cashew nuts, whose NPU matches sunflower

Tips for complementing the protein in nuts and seeds

1. **Amino Acid Makeup:** The amino acid pattern that emerges among the nuts and seeds is one of deficiency in the two **inside** columns, isoleucine and lysine, and strength in the two **outside** columns, tryptophan and the sulfur-containing amino acids. Sesame seed strikingly exemplifies this contrast. Seeds and many nuts therefore make good complements of legumes which have just the opposite pattern—as you recall from Table III.

Remember also the potential of dairy products to fill the amino acid "gaps" of nuts and seeds. The strength of dairy products in the two **inside** columns, isoleucine and lysine, means they have exactly what is needed by the nuts and seeds. It's not at all surprising, then, that experimentation has resulted in the following complementary combinations.

2. Experimentally determined complementary protein mixes include nuts and seeds: **For recipes see pages:**

plus Legumes, for example:

Peanuts* + Sesame + Soybeans	227–32
Sesame + Beans	215–19
Sesame + Soybeans + Wheat	189–94

plus Milk products, for example:

Peanuts + Milk	

plus Other nuts or seeds, for example:

Peanuts + Sunflower seeds	233–38

plus Grains (because grains and nuts and seeds are low in the same amino acids, their complementarity seems to usually depend on the presence of legumes or milk products), for example:

Peanuts + Wheat + Milk	239–47
Sesame + Wheat + Soybeans	189–94
Exception: Sesame + Rice	155–61

* Peanuts are botanically classified as legumes.

Table IV. NUTS AND SEEDS

Average Serving of Nuts and Seeds, Approx. 1 oz (28 g)	Percent of Daily Protein Allowance in an Average Serving		Ratings of Amino Acid Content as Compared to Egg Protein				Total Grams of Protein	NPU	Grams of Protein Your Body Can Use
	M	F	Tryp.	Iso.	Lys.	S.-C.			
	If complemented, add 3-4%			DEFICIENCY					
1. Pignolia nuts, 2½ tbsp	12	14	—¹	—	—	—	9	(~50)	5
2. Pumpkin and squash seeds, 2 tbsp	12	14	A	B	B	—	8	(~60)	5
	If complemented, add 2-3%								
3. Sunflower seeds, 3 tbsp, or sunflower meal, 4 tbsp	9	11	A	B	C	B	7	(58)	4
4. Peanuts, 2 tbsp	7	8	B	C	C	C²	8	(43)	3
5. Peanut butter, 2 tbsp	7	8	B	C	C	C²	8	(43)	3
6. Cashews, 12-16 nuts	7	8	A+	B	B	B	5	(58)	3
7. Sesame seeds, 3 tbsp, or sesame meal, 4 tbsp	7	8	A	C	C	A	5	(53)	3
8. Pistachio nuts, 3 tbsp	7	8	B	D	B	B²	5	(~50)	3
9. Black walnuts,³ 4 tbsp, 16-20 halves	7	8	B	C	D	B	6	(~50)	3
10. Brazil nuts, 8 medium	4	5	A+	C	D	A+	4	(50)	2

The following nuts are **not** good protein sources because they contain too many calories for the amount of protein you get: pecans chestnuts coconuts filberts hazelnuts macadamia nuts almonds pine nuts English walnuts. ³Black walnuts have about 40 percent more protein than English walnuts.

¹Amino acid content unknown. ²Also deficient in threonine.

seeds (and nearly equals soybeans). If you find that your favorite nuts (such as pecans or English walnuts) are not listed here, it's because they are too calorific! To illustrate: if you (a woman) wanted to get your daily protein allowance solely from pecans (hypothetical, of course), you would have to consume almost 1½ pounds of pecans which contain over 4000 calories—or about twice what you should consume. This illustrates the rationale I have used for including only those items which can provide protein without exceeding caloric needs. The one exception here is Brazil nuts which have been included because of their unusual strength in the sulfur-containing amino acids (rare in plant protein). For a complete analysis of the calorie "cost" of the foods given here, see Chart VIII which follows these tables.

Finally, notice that the portions given here are quite conservative. A 1-ounce serving of peanuts provides 7 to 8 percent of your daily protein needs. But, if you ate a 10-cent package of peanuts (1½ ounces) you would actually be fulfilling 10 to 12 percent of your daily allowance.

5. Grains, Cereals, and Their Products

Cereals provide almost half the protein in the world's diet. This might surprise you since the percent of protein in cereals is not high. Someone must be eating a lot of them! Not us, of course, but other people in the world.

Let's take a look at grains from several points of view. First, the *quantity* of protein they contain. Among the various grains we find wide differences. Wheat, rye, and oats have from 30 to 35 percent *more* protein by weight than rice, corn, barley, and millet. The protein content of one type of grain can also vary significantly: wheat, for example, ranges between 9 and 14 percent protein.

The values you find for wheat on the following tables (page 00–00) are based on the highest-protein wheat —hard red spring wheat. You may wish to check the labeling on wheat products to see what type of wheat is used. Durum wheat, often used in pasta, has the second highest protein content, 13 percent.

These differences may suggest to you that if rice is a staple in your diet you may wish to increase the protein content by adding some whole wheat, rye, or oats. Did you know that you can cook whole grain wheat, oats, and rye in the same way that you do rice? The mix has a nutty, rich flavor which you may prefer to rice alone.

Oatmeal is low (#8) on Table V only because we usually eat it in a rolled form that is much lighter than the whole grains. (Less weight: therefore, less protein.)

But what about the quality of cereal protein? Their NPU values generally range from the low 50s to the low 60s; but there are some important exceptions. The NPU of whole rice, 70, is probably the highest of any of the whole grains and equal to the NPU of beef! Wheat germ and rice germ (not listed) come next with NPUs of 67. Oatmeal and buckwheat follow with NPUs of 66 and 65, respectively. These values are higher than most vegetable protein and are comparable to the quality of beef. On the other hand, the lowest NPU of cereal products is that of wheat gluten (#2 under "Flour," page 90). Although gluten flour is 41 percent protein, its NPU of 39 means that only about *one-third* of its protein is available to the body. A deficiency of lysine (D rating) appears to be the culprit. These differences in quality and quantity among the grains mean that the price you pay and the calories you have to eat to get a given amount of protein also vary significantly. You may wish to take careful note of these differences on the cost and calorie charts (Charts VIII and IX) that follow. (See pages 102–3 and 115.)

Tips for complementing the protein in grains

1. **Amino Acid Makeup:** Like many nuts and seeds on the previous table, the amino acid deficiencies of cereals generally appear in the two **inside** columns (isoleucine and lysine) of Table V. (This pattern is broken primarily by processed cereal products and by legume flours that I have included here only for convenience.) As we have already noted, legumes are the obvious match for grains because they have the reverse pattern of deficiencies. Except for blackeye peas and mung beans, legumes are moderately strong in the second column, isoleucine; and without exception legumes are very strong in the third column, lysine. Perhaps the simplest way to regularly use legumes to complement grains is merely to add about two tablespoons of soy grits (partially cooked, cracked soybeans) to every cup of grain—in any dish from your morning oatmeal to your supper casserole. The dish will taste better too. Certain commercial cereals such as "Protein Plus" have already added soy grits for you. So, be sure to check the labels of commercially made cereals for a fortuitous complementary protein combination!

For the same reasons—strengths in both center columns, isoleucine and lysine—milk products make good complements to grains. But there's a "natural" complement that you might not notice. Yeast, on Table VII (page 96), is also well endowed with these two amino acids in which grains are deficient. Nutritional or brewer's yeast, as it is called, can be mixed into breads and pancakes or sprinkled on breakfast cereals.

2. Experimentally determined complementary protein mixes include grains:

<table>
<tr><td></td><td>For recipes
see pages:</td></tr>
<tr><td>plus Legumes, for example:</td><td></td></tr>
<tr><td>Rice + Legumes</td><td>133–39</td></tr>
</table>

Corn + Legumes	195–201
Wheat + Legumes	176–80
	For recipes see pages:

plus Milk products, for example:

Rice + Milk	162–68
Wheat + Cheese	169–75
Wheat + Milk	169–75

plus Nuts and seeds (because grains and nuts and seeds are low in the same amino acids, their complementarity seems to usually depend on the presence of legumes or milk products), for example:

Wheat + Peanut + Milk	239–47
Wheat + Sesame + Soybean	189–94
Exception: Rice + Sesame	155–61

plus Yeast, for example:

Brewer's Yeast + Rice	151–54

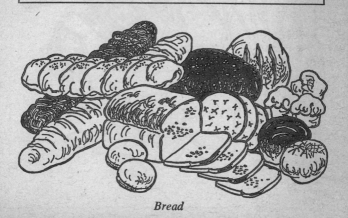

Bread

Wheat

Cereal products such as bulgur (#4 on Table V) may stump you if you've only read traditional cookbooks. Bulgur is partially cooked, cracked wheat. Its processing is both an asset and a liability. Thus, while the lysine in bulgur is more available than that in whole wheat, from 2 to 28 percent of its B vitamins are destroyed. For recipe ideas using bulgur turn to Part IV, Section B (page 220).

6. Vegetables

A glance at the following table will show you that vegetables, in general, will not be large contributors to your daily protein intake. On a moisture-free basis, some green vegetables have a protein content equivalent to nuts, seeds, and beans. But their water content gives them bulk that limits their usefulness in our diets—as protein suppliers, that is. However, don't forget their valuable role in providing essential vitamins and minerals! So, if you enjoy these vegetables, eat lots of them. Whereas I have given one-half cup of cooked greens as an average serving, you may enjoy twice this amount. With the exception of potato, all these vegetables are low in calories; so there is no need to limit your intake on this account.

The NPU scores of these vegetables provide some interesting surprises. Among the legumes in Table III (page 78), we saw that mung beans had an NPU of 57. But here as mung bean sprouts their NPU is only 36. Soybean sprouts also take a slight dip in NPU, with 56 as compared to 61 for the dried bean.

To increase the protein content and taste interest of vegetable dishes, experiment with milk- and cheese-based sauces. I've discovered that buttermilk makes an excellent sauce base. Since it is already somewhat thick, one needn't add as much flour. In addition, its tartness

Table V. GRAINS, CEREALS, AND THEIR PRODUCTS

Average Serving of Grains and Cereals¹	Percent of Daily Protein Allowance in an Average Serving		Ratings of Amino Acid Content as Compared to Egg Protein				Total Grams of Protein	NPU	Grams of Protein Your Body Can Use
	M	F	Tryp.	Iso.	Lys.	S.-C.			
	If complemented, add 2-3%			DEFICIENCY →	→				
1. Wheat, whole grain hard red spring, ⅓ c (55-60 g)	12	15	B	C	C	B	8	(60)	5
2. Rye, whole grain, ⅓ c (55-60 g)	9	11	C	C	C	B	7	(58)	4
3. Egg noodles, cooked tender, 1 c (160 g)	9	11	B	B	C	C	7	(~60)	4
4. Bulgur (parboiled wheat), ⅓ c (50-55 g), or cracked wheat cereal, ⅓ c (35-40 g)	9	11	B	C	C	B	6	(~60)	4
5. Barley, pot or Scotch, ⅓ c (60-65 g)	9	11	A	C	C	B	6	(60)	4
6. Millet, ⅓ c (55-60 g)	7	8	A+	B	C	A	6	(~55)	3
7. Spaghetti or macaroni cooked tender, 1 c (140-150 g)	7	8	B	B	C	C	5	(~50)	3

Average Serving of Grains and Cereals[1]	Percent of Daily Protein Allowance in an Average Serving		Ratings of Amino Acid Content as Compared to Egg Protein				Total Grams of Protein	NPU	Grams of Protein Your Body Can Use
	M	F	Tryp.	Iso.	Lys.	S.-C.[1]			
				DEFICIENCY ➡	➡				
8. Oatmeal, ⅓ c (30-35 g)	7	8	B	Ⓒ	Ⓒ	B	4	(66)	3
9. Rice, ⅓ c (60-65 g)									
a. Brown	7	8	B	Ⓒ	Ⓒ	B	5	(70)	3
b. Parboiled (converted)	7	8	B	B	Ⓒ	A	5	(~70)	3
c. Milled, polished	5	6	A	B	Ⓒ	B	4	(57)	2
10. Wheat germ, commercial, 2 level tbsp (11-12 g)	5	6	Ⓒ	B	A+	B	3	(67)	2
11. Bread, commercial, 1 slice, whole wheat or rye	2	3	—	—	—	—	2.4	(~45)	1.2
12. Wheat bran, crude, 2 round tbsp (10 g)	2	3	A	Ⓒ	B	A	1.6	(55)	0.9

[1]Raw unless otherwise stated.

FLOUR

For ease in calculating the amount of protein in the bread you make, protein values for flours are given here per cup rather than per average serving

One Cup of Flour	Ratings of Amino Acid Content as Compared to Egg Protein				Total Grams of Protein	NPU	Grams of Protein Your Body Can Use	If complemented, add usable grams [1]
	Tryp.	Iso.	Lys.	S.-C.				
		DEFICIENCY →	→					
1. Soybean flour, defatted (138 g)	A	B	A	C [2]	65	(61)	40	5
2. Gluten flour (140 g)	B	B	D	B [3]	85	(39)	23	?
3. Peanut flour, defatted (100 g)	B	C	C	C	48	(43)	21	9
4. Soybean flour, full fat (72 g)	A	B	A	C	26	(61)	16	3
5. Whole wheat flour, or cracked wheat cereal (120 g) (see Appendix F for comparison with white flour)	B	C	D	B	16	(60)	10	2

One Cup of Flour	Ratings of Amino Acid Content as Compared to Egg Protein				Total Grams of Protein	NPU	Grams of Protein Your Body Can Use	If complemented, add usable grams[1]
	Tryp.	Iso.	Lys.	S.-C.				
		DEFICIENCY						
6. Rye flour, dark[4] (119 g)	C	C	C	B	16	(58)	9	2
7. Buckwheat flour, dark[4] (100 g)	B	C	C	B	12	(65)	8	2
8. Oatmeal (80 g)	B	C	C	B	11	(66)	7	1
9. Barley flour (112 g)	B	C	C	B	11	(60)	7	2
10. Cornmeal, whole ground (118 g)	C	C	C	B	10	(51)	5	2
11. Wheat bran, crude (55 g)	A	C	B	A	9	(55)	5	1

[1]Approximate amount of protein saved by complementing the protein in the flour. Refer to the beginning of Table V for tips on complementing grain protein.

[2]Also slightly deficient in valine.

[3]Also deficient in threonine.

[4]Both dark rye and dark buckwheat flours have almost twice as much protein as the light varieties.

Table VI. VEGETABLES

Average Serving of Vegetables Based on a Fresh, Uncooked Weight of 3½ oz (100 g)[1]	Percent Daily Protein Allowance in an Average Serving		Ratings of Amino Acid Content as Compared to Egg Protein				Total Grams of Protein	NPU	Grams of Protein Your Body Can Use
	M	F	Tryp.	Iso.	Lys.	S.-C.			
	If complemented, add 2-5%		DEFICIENCY	DEFICIENCY →		DEFICIENCY →			
1. Lima beans, green, 4 rounded tbsp. about ½ c when cooked	9	11	A	A	A	D	8	(~52)	4
2. Soybean sprouts, 1 c	7	8		C	C	F	6	(56)	3
3. Peas, green, ¾ c shelled	7	8	B	B	A+	D	6	(53)	3
4. Brussels sprouts, 9 med.	7	8	B	B	A-	D	5	(<60)[2]	3
5. Corn, one medium ear	7	8	D	D	C	B	4	(72)	3
Add 1-2%									
6. Broccoli, 1 stalk, 5½ in.	5	6	B	B	B	C	4	(<60)	2-3
7. Kale, w/stems, ¾ c when cooked	5	6	B	C	C	D	4	(54)	2
8. Collards, ½ c when cooked	5	6	A	C	A	C	4	(~45)	2
9. Mushrooms, 10 small, 4 large	5	6	B	D D	B	A[3]	3	(72)	2
10. Asparagus, 5-6 spears	3	4	B	D	B	D	3	(<60)	1.8
11. Artichoke, ½ large bud	3	4				—	3	(<60)	1.8
12. Cauliflower, 1 c flower pieces	3	4	A	B	A	D	3	(<60)	1.8

Average Serving of Vegetables Based on a Fresh, Uncooked Weight of 3½ oz (100 g)[1]	Percent Daily Protein Allowance in an Average Serving		Ratings of Amino Acid Content as Compared to Egg Protein				Total Grams of Protein	NPU	Grams of Protein Your Body Can Use
	M	F	Tryp.	Iso.	Lys.	S.-C.			
				DEFICIENCY		DEFICIENCY			
13. Spinach, ½ c when cooked	Add 1-2%		A	→B	A+	→B	3	(~50)	1.5
14. Turnip greens, ½ c when cooked	3	4	A	C	B	D	3	(45)	1.4
15. Mung bean sprouts, 1 c (100 g)	3	4	—	—	—	—	4	(36)	1.4
16. Mustard greens, ½ c when cooked	3	4	A+	C	B	C	3	(~45)	1.4
17. Potato, white, ½ med. baking potato	3	3	A	C	B	D	2	(60)	1.2
18. Okra, 8-9 pods, 3 in. long	2	3	B	B	B	C	2	(<60)	1.2
19. Chard, 3/5 c when cooked	2	3	B	B	B	—	2	(~50)	1

[1] Shopping hint: 100 g (or 3½ oz) is equivalent to slightly less than ¼ lb on the grocery scale.
[2] Where the NPU of a vegetable is unknown I have judged it to be less than 60 (<60), based on typical NPU scores of other vegetables.
[3] The S.-C. content of mushrooms is disputed in my sources. I chose the high (A) level because it is in line with the unusually high NPU (72) of mushrooms.

Tips for complementing the protein in fresh vegetables

Since the most striking feature of fresh vegetables is their very low ratings in the last amino acid column (sulfur-containing amino acids), you would first want to look for foods with a high rating in that column. In Table IV (page 81), we find **sesame seed** and **Brazil nuts** —both unusually strong (A rating) in the last column. Sesame and Brazils would probably serve best as complements to those fresh vegetables such as lima beans, green peas, Brussels sprouts, and cauliflower which are very deficient in the last column while strong (A or B rating) in the second column (isoleucine). This is true because sesame and Brazils are themselves somewhat weak (C rating) in the second column.

In Table V among the grains we can also find some possible complements to these fresh vegetables. **Millet** and **parboiled rice** (converted) stand out as exceptions among the grains. They are both very strong (A rating) in the last column (sulfur-containing) and moderately strong (B rating) in the second column (isoleucine). They, therefore, might well complement the protein in many fresh vegetables, especially the greens, which have just the opposite pattern. See page 133 for a recipe combining fresh greens and rice.

Some vegetables might complement the protein in other vegetables. **Mushrooms,** high (A rating) in the last column (sulfur-containing), could be combined with lima beans, green peas, Brussels sprouts, broccoli, or cauliflower—all lacking in this amino acid.

highlights many green vegetables. Look for the recipe for easy-to-make Buttermilk Hollandaise Sauce in the section on low-fat dairy products, Section E.

Also, sliced or crumbled hard-boiled egg is very tasty on green vegetables such as spinach or asparagus. Adding nuts is another way to increase the protein value of vegetable dishes. Your favorite vegetable dishes in Chinese restaurants probably include walnuts or cashews. Why not do the same? Broccoli, peas, and cauliflower are especially good with nuts.

The following vegetables can*not* be considered protein sources because they contain less than 2 percent protein. Many, however, should be included in the diet as sources of vitamins and minerals: snap beans, beets, burdock, cabbage, eggplant, lettuce, onions, green peppers, pumpkin, radishes, rhubarb, squash, sweet potatoes, tomatoes, and turnips.

7. Nutritional Additives

If you have doubts about the adequacy of your protein intake, even a small amount of the first two items in the Nutritional Additives table can give you a real protein boost. Only one tablespoon of dried egg white or one-fourth cup of "Tiger's Milk" mixed into your favorite drink can fill 12 to 25 percent of your daily protein need.

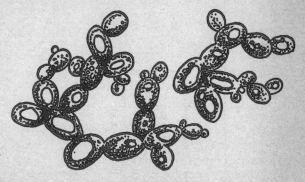

Yeast patterns

Table VII. NUTRITIONAL ADDITIVES

Average Serving of Nutritional Additive	Percent of Daily Protein Allowance in an Average Serving		Ratings of Amino Acid Content as Compared to Egg Protein				Total Grams of Protein	NPU	Grams of Protein Your Body Can Use
	M	F	Tryp.	Iso.	Lys.	S.-C.			
					STRENGTH →				
1. Egg white, dried, powdered, ½ oz (14 g)	21	25	A+	B	A+	A+	11	(83)	9
2. "Tiger's Milk," ¼ c, ½ oz (14 g)	12	14	–	–	–	–	7	(~75)	5
3. Brewer's yeast, powder, 1 level tbsp, (9–10 g)	5	6	B	A	A+	C	4	(50)	2
4. Wheat germ, commercial, 2 level tbsp, (11–12 g)	5	6	C	B	A+	B	3	(67)	2

Tips for complementing other foods with the protein in these nutritional additives

Amino acid strength in the two center columns (isoleucine and especially, lysine) make these nutritional additives likely complements for foods having the opposite amino acid pattern. Likely complementary protein combinations include nutritional additives:

See Table:

plus Certain nuts and seeds, for example:

sesame seed, black walnuts   IV

plus Many grains, for example:

wheat, barley, oatmeal, rice   V

An experimentally determined complementary protein combination is nutritional yeast: For recipes

see pages:

plus Rice: 151–54

The other two nutritional additives (#3 and #4 in Table VII) are used by most people because of their high vitamin and mineral content. (Yeast is from two to ten times richer than wheat germ in these nutrients.) I have included them because a very small amount (one or two tablespoons) can meet 5 percent of your protein allowance and, secondly, because of their amino acid strengths.

8. For Comparison: Meat and Poultry

Notice that only 3½ ounces of meat contribute from 30 to 61 percent of your daily protein allowance. These figures make very clear that the enormous quantities of meat we now consume are hardly needed! In Eastern cuisine small amounts of meat supplement staple vegetable dishes. This dietary tradition, although perhaps

Turkeys

Table VIII. MEAT AND POULTRY

Average Serving of Meat and Poultry, Cooked, 3½ oz (100 g)	Percent of Daily Protein Allowance in an Average Serving		Ratings of Amino Acid Content as Compared to Egg Protein				Total Grams of Protein	NPU	Grams of Protein Your Body Can Use
	M	F	Tryp.	Iso.	Lys.	S.-C.			
					STRENGTH				
1. Turkey, roasted, 3 slices, 3X2½X¼"	50	61	—	B	A+	B	31	(~70)	22
2. Pork, loin chop, lean and fat	44	53	A	A	A+	B¹	29	(~67)	19
3. Porterhouse steak, lean and marbled only (½ lb raw)	39	47	B	B	A+	B¹	25	(67)	17
4. Hamburger, medium (½ lb raw)	39	47	B	B	A+	B¹	26	(67)	17
5. Chicken, fryer, breast	35	42	B	A	A+	B	23	(~65)	15
6. Lamb, rib chop, lean and fat	30	36	B	B	A+	B¹	20	(~65)	13

¹Also slightly deficient in valine.

determined by the limited availability of meat, more correctly reflects the body's actual needs.

Gelatin, an animal protein, is often recommended as a protein supplement. Actually, it should be your last choice. Several important amino acids are virtually lacking in gelatin. It has an NPU of 2! Moreover, gelatin can *reduce* the usability of the protein in food eaten with it.

Tips for using meat and poultry to complement the protein in plant food

1. High amino acid ratings (especially lysine) give even small portions of meat and poultry the ability to complement plant foods, particularly those, such as grains, which are low in lysine.

2. Turkey apparently surpasses all other meat and poultry in its ability to complement plant protein. Experiments show that if you add only one-fifth as much turkey to a meal of wheat, peanuts, or blackeye peas, the protein quality of the combination will be the same as if the entire meal had been beef! [69]

D. Getting the Most Protein for the Least Calories

Chart VIII (page 102–3) tells you the number of calories you have to consume in order to get 1 gram of usable protein from selected food sources. The term "usable protein" means that the protein content has been reduced according to the NPU of the food.

You are all aware of the fact that being overweight is in some way associated with higher risks of dying. (Or, if you're not, you might ask a life insurance salesman. I'm sure he would know!) What might be less familiar to you is the fact that American men who are only *10 percent* overweight eventually exhibit a *20 percent* greater risk of dying before their time than do men of normal weight.[70] Thus, even a modest increase in body weight involves much more than a question of looking good. It is a question of good health. So this guide is for those who wish to stay within calorie bounds without jeopardizing protein intake.

Recall that the calorie "cost" was one of the criteria used in selecting good protein sources. With few exceptions, only those foods which can give you enough protein without exceeding your daily caloric needs have been included. In Appendix B you'll find the exact number of calories per gram of usable protein for each food item.

Now, let's look at Chart VIII. Notice that as you trace food items down the chart, the number of calories increases. Arrayed across the chart are the nonmeat food groups chosen as good protein sources. As you read from left to right, the average calorie "cost" of the items in each group increases—seafood being the least calorific, while seeds and nuts have the highest calorie cost.[71] Thus, it is easy to see how the food groups compare as calorie contributors. Now let's take each food group and discuss its special features—from a calorie point of view.

1. Seafood

Seafood is inevitably in first place. It could hardly miss. Two items in this group, haddock and cod, are essentially pure protein. Every gram of protein itself contains 4 calories. Therefore 4 calories per gram of protein is the minimum that any food could have. (Each

CHART VIII

CALORIE "COST" PER GRAM

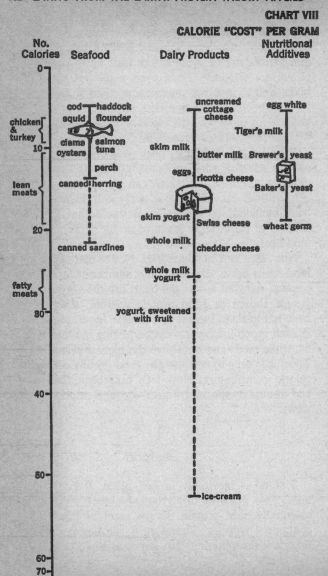

No. Calories	Seafood	Dairy Products	Nutritional Additives
0			
	cod — haddock	uncreamed cottage cheese	egg white
chicken & turkey	squid flounder		Tiger's milk
	clams salmon	skim milk	Brewer's yeast
10	oysters tuna	butter milk	
	perch	eggs ricotta cheese	Baker's yeast
lean meats	canned herring		
		skim yogurt Swiss cheese	wheat germ
20		whole milk cheddar cheese	
	canned sardines		
		whole milk yogurt	
fatty meats		yogurt, sweetened with fruit	
30			
40			
50		ice-cream	
60			
70			
80			

OF USABLE PROTEIN

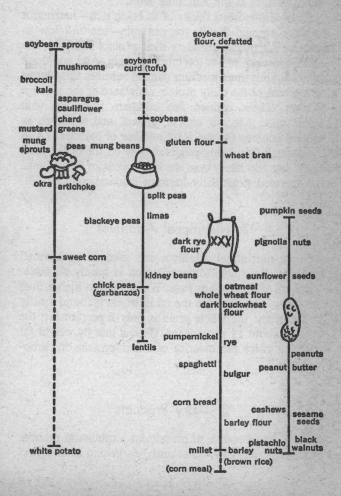

Vegetables	Legumes	Grains & Flours	Seeds & Nuts

soybean sprouts

soybean flour, defatted

mushrooms

soybean curd (tofu)

broccoli
kale

asparagus
cauliflower
chard

mustard greens

soybeans

mung sprouts   peas mung beans

gluten flour

wheat bran

okra artichoke

split peas

blackeye peas limas

pumpkin seeds

dark rye flour XXX

pignolia nuts

sweet corn

kidney beans

sunflower seeds

chick peas (garbanzos)

oatmeal
whole wheat flour
dark buckwheat flour

pumpernickel rye

lentils

spaghetti

peanuts

peanut butter

bulgur

corn bread

cashews
sesame seeds

barley flour

white potato

millet barley

pistachio nuts

black walnuts

(corn meal) (brown rice)

gram of pure carbohydrate also contains 4 calories while each gram of fat has 9 calories. Thus, by weight, fats have over twice as many calories as protein or carbohydrates.) Since haddock and cod contain no carbohydrates and an almost immeasurable amount of fat, they are right at the minimum level.

Even seafood one thinks of as being rich—herring or sardines canned in oil, for example—are *still* low in calories when one considers their protein strength. The trick is just not to eat too much of them. And you don't need to. Only four medium canned sardines fills almost 20 percent of the daily protein allowance of the average woman. These canned fish compare favorably with whole milk, cheddar cheese, greens, and soybeans as protein sources for the least number of calories. (And these small fish, being relatively low on the ocean food chain, are less likely than the large predator fish to have accumulated potentially harmful contaminants.)

2. Nutritional Additives

Since nutritional additives are used in such small amounts, their caloric contribution is hardly an issue. They are all low, in any case. Wheat germ is higher than the others only because the oil in wheat is found mostly in the germ: the whole grain is only 2 percent fat; the germ is about 11 percent fat. (Recall that by weight fat contains twice the calories of either protein or carbohydrates.)

3. Dairy Products

As a major source of protein for a minimum number of calories, dairy products rank just behind seafood. As with some fish, uncreamed cottage cheese can also be called practically pure protein (except for its water content, of course). It is less than 1 percent fat and only 3 percent carbohydrate.

Notice that skim milk and buttermilk have fewer calories per gram of usable protein than even plain yogurt. For your convenience and pleasure a special section on interesting ways to use low-fat dairy products follows this discussion, Section E. But notice here that commercial, sweetened yogurt, advertised as a good "diet" food, is not in fact outstanding as a low-calorie source of protein: it places well down the chart.

One tends to think of cheese as calorie laden because we are aware of its high fat content (26 to 30 percent fat). So you might well be surprised to find cheeses ranking near yogurt and whole milk on this chart. The answer is their extraordinarly high protein content. Cheese is from 18 to 36 percent protein as compared to only 4 percent for milk! This means that you need eat only a very small amount. A 2-ounce piece of cheese supplies about 30 percent of your daily protein allowance, but only about 10 percent (200 calories) of the average woman's calorie allowance.

4. Vegetables

Fresh vegetables rate well on this scale for exactly the opposite reason as does cheese. Their fat content is virtually zero but their protein content is not high either, so you have to eat lots of them to get a significant amount of protein. But that's all right—calorie-wise. You would have to eat three-quarters of a pound of broccoli, for example, before you would consume the number of calories contained in a 1-inch cube of cheese.

But even among these low-calorie vegetables there are

some real differences. Soybean sprouts, mushrooms, and broccoli have about half as many calories for every gram of usable protein as do peas and okra. Sweet corn contributes more calories than all of these and the potato is right at the calorie limit for a good protein source.

5. Legumes

From a caloric point of view, we find wide variability among legumes. Soybean curd (tofu) has the fewest calories for the amount of usable protein, largely because most of the fat is removed in its processing. Tofu is truly an excellent protein source. Lightly sautéed with a fresh vegetable accompaniment, one could easily eat 7 ounces of tofu and fulfill 25 to 30 percent of a day's need for protein—at the cost of only about 5 to 7 percent of a day's calorie allotment. I've included several tofu dishes among the recipes given later in this book.

But the wide variation among the dried legumes is not due to differential fat content, or even to the amount of protein contained (except for soybeans, whose protein content is well above the others). The wide range reflects primarily differences in protein *quality*. Lentils, for example, place far down the scale because they have the lowest NPU score. Low NPU means less usable protein. The result is that you or I have to eat more of the food (and hence more calories) to get a given amount of protein.

Legumes are another category of food (like cheese) that many people think of as being "fattening." Yet, in relation to the amount of protein you are getting, soybeans actually are on a par with green vegetables! Most of the legumes have between one-half and two-thirds of the maximum allowable calories per gram of usable protein. And this is pretty good. It means that you could, conceivably, eat all of your daily protein allowance in the form of legumes and still have left one-half to one-third of your daily calorie allowance for other good things.

6. Grains and Flours

Part of the reason for the wide range here in calories per gram of usable protein is that I've included some legume flours with the grains—since they too are used in baking. Defatted soybean flour is the clearcut winner with only 11 calories per gram of usable protein, making it similar to skim milk from the calorie-to-protein point of view. Gluten flour would be quite near it, if it weren't for its low NPU score. Gluten's low quality reduces the amount of usable protein—causing it to drop to the level of whole milk or cheddar cheese.

The variability among the true whole grains and their products is for the most part attributable to differences in protein content; that is, their percent on a weight basis. For this reason, you would have to eat more calories to get a given amount of protein from barley, millet, rice, or cornmeal than you would from dark rye, oatmeal, or whole wheat. In fact, judged by the calorie criterion I have adopted, cornmeal and rice should not be considered as good protein sources at all! Rice has about 69 calories per gram of usable protein, and cornmeal has approximately 80. I have included both because they are so widely eaten as protein sources. To compensate for their failings, I encourage their use in combination with other foods that increase both their protein content (such as egg in cornbread) and their protein quality (rice plus beans, for example).

Sesame seed, flower and pod

7. Nuts and Seeds

The nuts and seeds are all located on the lower half of the chart, meaning that they all have between 30 and 60 calories per gram of usable protein. But, like cheese and legumes, these particular seeds and nuts are so rich in protein that, even with a high fat content, they are no more calorific per gram of usable protein than are the whole grains. (Many nuts have been excluded because their calorie to usable protein ratio exceeds 60:1. These are listed at the end of Table IV, page 81.)

You might be surprised to see sunflower seeds and sesame seeds so widely separated on the chart, sesame having significantly more calories per gram of usable protein than sunflower seeds (57 compared to 40). The reason is threefold. In comparison with sunflower seeds, sesame seed has a slightly higher fat content, a 20 percent lower protein content, and a lower NPU score.

E. Delicious Ways To Enjoy Low-Fat Dairy Products

Many people are reluctant to increase their use of dairy products as a source of protein. Aware of the high fat content of some dairy foods, they avoid them for fear of gaining weight. Others are particularly concerned about cholesterol and think that, on this ground, they must limit their dairy intake. (In fact, most cheese has only about 20 percent more cholesterol than most meat; and whole milk, on a weight basis, has six times *less* cholesterol than meat.) Still others, aware that pesticide residues accumulate in animal fat, spurn dairy products in order to avoid ingesting these contaminants.

But whether it is calories, cholesterol or environmental contaminants that you wish to avoid, there is no need to forego the pleasures of dairy foods—not when there are so many delicious ways to enjoy low-fat dairy products! Because they have been relegated to the low status of "diet foods" in our culture the culinary potential of low-fat dairy products is largely unexplored. It is not surprising, then, that several of the best ideas for enjoying these foods originate in other cultures.

Here are a few suggestions for using low-fat dairy products that will increase the taste interest of your diet while providing protein *and* saving you calories!

1. Buttermilk

a. As a Fruit Freeze: A common drink in India is known as a "lassi," basically a foamy mixture of crushed ice, yogurt, and sugar. If you have a blender you can make an American version of this light refresher. I've suggested using buttermilk mainly because it is so much cheaper. Both yogurt and buttermilk work equally well. Just put in a blender about 1½ cups of crushed ice, ⅔ cups of buttermilk, and sugar to taste (not too much because the slight tartness is very pleasing). Add your favorite fresh fruit. Banana and pineapple is an especially tasty combination. Or merely squeeze half a lemon or tangerine into the mixture. Blend on low, then high speed, until the mixture is foamy and the ice is like snow. There is nothing more refreshing!

b. As a Cold Dessert or Breakfast Sauce: Mix applesauce with buttermilk to make a thick sauce for sweet, spicy cakes. This mixture is especially delicious on cornbread. With brown sugar buttermilk tastes good on breakfast cereals—perhaps better on oat than wheat cereal, however. Buttermilk can also make an "instant" rice pudding out of leftover cold rice. Just add brown sugar, raisins, and chopped nuts.

c. As a Dinner Sauce with Vegetables: Melt a small amount of butter in the top of a double boiler and add about 1 tbsp flour, ¼ tsp mustard powder, ½ tsp salt, and a dash of pepper and paprika. Mix well, cooking 1 to 2 minutes. Add 1 cup of buttermilk, stirring. Have a beaten egg ready and use a whisk to stir it in. Cook until it is the consistency you like and adjust the seasoning. This sauce is perfect for green vegetables like asparagus and broccoli.

2. Yogurt

a. As a Cheese Spread: In Lebanon and elsewhere in the Middle East a common way to eat yogurt is called "labneh." Essentially "labneh" is yogurt from which the water has been drained so that it develops the consistency of sour cream. (Note that sour cream has about 82 calories per gram of usable protein while yogurt has less than 20.)

Here's how to make it: The traditional method is to make a small muslin bag about 6 by 8 inches with a draw-string closing. (You might use scraps from an old sheet and a rubber band closing.) Simply pour in about a pint of yogurt and hang the bag over the sink (or anyplace that could receive the water dripping from the yogurt). (Do *not* stir yogurt before pouring it into the bag.) Leave it overnight and the next day you'll have "labneh." A less authentic method is to lay the cloth in a collander, pour in the yogurt, tie the cloth, and place it all in a bigger bowl to drain.

b. As a Multipurpose Sauce in Cooking: As you will see in the recipe section, yogurt makes a delicious addition to many recipes, especially Indian and Middle Eastern vegetable and legume dishes. Of course it is also a tasty dessert topping, particularly for spicy puddings like Indian Pudding.

3. Ricotta Cheese

a. As a Light Cheese Spread for Bread: Recall from the previous charts that ricotta cheese has only 14 calories per gram of usable protein which makes it an even lower calorie source of protein than low-fat yogurt. For the protein you are getting it is also several times cheaper! Ricotta cheese has a light taste and pleasing consistency for use as a spread on bread. My favorite breakfast toast always has a thick layer of ricotta and a little orange marmalade on top. For even more protein, add chopped nuts and, for sweetness, add chopped dates. This spread is extra good on Boston Brown Bread. See Part IV, Section B, combination 12.

b. As a Creamy Cheese in Cooking: Ricotta can be thinned with a little milk or yogurt and used as you would sour cream in cooking. An example is Rice con Queso, a recipe in combination 6, in Part IV, Section B. Of course, ricotta is the traditional cheese to be used in Italian dishes such as lasagne and manicotti. And, it can be added to pancakes, or seasoned and used to fill blintze-like pancakes. The possibilities are infinite!

4. Cottage Cheese

a. As a Quick Snack: Since only 6 tbsp of cottage cheese can fill one-third of your daily protein allowance, it deserves some special attention. For an easily made snack, it can be mixed with a little applesauce and cinnamon (chopped nuts too, if you like). It is also good with chopped chives and a juicy sliced tomato.

Peanuts grow underground

b. As a Party Dip: Cottage cheese, made smooth in a blender, can serve as the basis of delicious dips. My favorite includes minced clams, chopped onions, and a little thyme.

c. As a Cheese Cake: If rich cheese cake always tempts you, here is your salvation. Blend until smooth: 1 pound cottage cheese, 1 cup lemon yogurt, 3 egg yolks, 1 tsp vanilla, 1 tbsp lemon juice and the rind of one lemon, ½ cup honey, ¼ tsp salt, and ¼ cup wholewheat flour. Fold in stiffly beaten egg whites (3), and pour into a 9-inch graham cracker crust. Bake in a medium oven until the center is firm. Loosen cake from sides of pan but let it cool before removing. (A spring-form pan is by far the easiest to use.) Serve with fresh berries.

d. As a Dinner "Soufflé": See the recipe for cheese-noodle "soufflé" in combination 7, Part IV, Section B.

F. Your Protein Dollar: A Cost Comparison

The protein cost chart (Chart IX, page 115), tells you how much it would cost to fill all of a day's protein allowance from a single food source eaten alone.* The prices are based on the grams of protein in the food, with an adjustment for protein quality. In other words, the price is based on the grams of protein your body can *use*, not on the total grams of protein. Of course, the chart is for the purpose of comparison. I'm not expecting you to eat your daily protein allowance in only one food!

---

* The cost is based on 43.1 grams of *usable* protein, the daily allowance for the average American male weighing 154 pounds. "Usable" protein means that the total grams of protein have been reduced by the NPU score to the level the body can actually use.

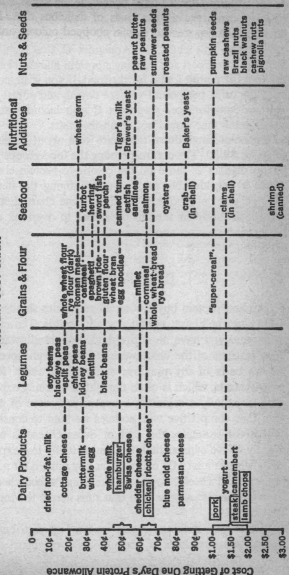

CHART IX
PROTEIN COST CHART

Although prices fluctuate with the state of the economy and vary throughout the countrty, these changes would undoubtedly not alter the basic pattern that emerges on this chart. In Appendix C I've included both the exact cost for one day's protein allowance and the cost per pound I paid for the food. If you wish, compare the price per pound you are paying and adjust for any major difference. Appendix C also includes additional items that would not fit on the chart.

The costs range down the chart from about 10 cents to about $2.50. The contrast among the food groups are not as distinct as those on the calorie-to-protein chart. There is considerably more overlap among the items. This calls for even closer scrutiny of the chart. Let us take each group in turn in order not to overlook any critical information about protein price.

1. Dairy Products:

The best protein buy among all categories stands out clearly on the chart: nonfat dry milk solids. Ten cents a day and you have an entire day's protein allowance! Two features of the chart were completely unexpected on the basis of my previous assumptions about food costs: cheese, which is often thought of as being expensive, is actually a relatively *in*expensive source of protein. It is competitive with sources we tend to consider cheap; for example, the cost of Swiss cheese is only slightly above canned tuna fish and actually less expensive than peanuts! (Of course, you pay quite a bit more for presliced cheese. So if you like thinly sliced cheese, try a cheese slicer—the kind that runs across the top of the cheese.)

The second striking feature in the cost distribution among dairy products is the high price of yogurt as a source of protein. You might as well be eating steak! Now, if you were to make yogurt yourself, starting with dried skim milk, it would be about fifteen times cheaper than commercially made yogurt.* Aside from the fact that yogurt costs about three times more than milk, yogurt from skim milk has about 15 percent *less* protein than fortified skim milk, and yogurt from whole milk has 25 percent less protein.

2. Legumes

Legumes are a uniformly low-cost source of protein, even after taking into consideration their low quality. Soybeans placed first in three categories on the calorie-to-protein chart, and here on the cost chart they rate second, very close indeed to nonfat skim milk solids. This is partly because soybeans are not considered to be fit for human consumption. The happy result for the consumer is that he doesn't have to pay for the artificial cost of advertising. (The drawback of course is that most people still think that this extraordinary source of protein is inedible!)

3. Grains and Flour

The price of a day's protein allowance from most of the grains and their products ranges between 20 and 70 cents—with wheat and rye at the low end and millet and cornmeal at the high end. This positioning reflects both the higher quality and quantity of protein in wheat, rye, and oats. As you can see, they are as cheap a source of protein as the legumes.

I have included the commercial cereal "Roman Meal" to show that such products can sometimes be less ex-

* See directions on p. 269 of *The Natural Foods Cookbook*.

pensive than staples like cornmeal. In this case the low protein-price is due to processed flaxseed, a very high-protein oilseed, contained in "Roman Meal." But, as you know, not all commercial cereals are a bargain. Look at "Super-Cereal." It is in the same protein price category as meat!

4. Seafood

Certain seafoods are a real cost surprise: Tuna, that old cheap-meal standby, is actually more expensive than swordfish, and only about 14 cents cheaper than salmon. And crab, often reserved for only the most special meal, is only slightly more expensive than peanuts! But the least expensive of the fish, such as perch, cod, or turbot, are as cheap a means of getting one's daily protein allowance as beans.

5. Nutritional Additives

"Tiger's Milk," a commercial mixture of milk and soy protein, rates very favorably among the nutritional additives. On the grocery shelf, selling at 99 cents for ½ pound, it appears quite expensive. But, according to its label, "Tiger's Milk" is 50 percent protein, greater than any naturally occurring protein in food. This high protein content puts it in the protein price bracket of milk or wheat bran.

Brewer's yeast is also very reasonable (on a par with peanut butter, for example)—especially considering the fact that it is a superb source of B vitamins and also rich in minerals over and above its use as a protein contributor.

6. Nuts and Seeds

In this food group we find some of the highest priced protein sources. Pistachio nuts in the shell are off the chart altogether, costing about $5.00 for a day's protein quota. But don't shun such delights as cashews and black walnuts because they're costly—just use them sparingly. Only a small amount can turn the simplest vegetable recipe into a special dish. But the only really good buys are peanuts and the seeds.

Another point worth noticing is the difference between the roasted and raw forms of the same nut. Raw peanuts and raw cashews (at least as they are sold in health food stores in the San Francisco Bay area) are significantly cheaper than their roasted counterparts (as much as $1 a pound cheaper for cashews!).

Pumpkin and Squash

Part IV

Combining Non-Meat Foods to Increase Protein Values

Rice

A. It Pays To Mix Your Own

We have come this far on the basis of a great many facts and statistics. Now, in bringing these ideas into our daily lives, we come to the truly pleasurable part—the pleasure of good eating! But by now many of you may well fear that my appeal for a more rational use of our earth will only take the pleasure out of eating and make of it a terribly complicated, even dull, affair. Certainly not! Experiment a little and both your palate and your creative sense will likely tell you the opposite.

Here you'll discover food combinations in which the essential amino acids lacking in one food are made up for by those present in another food. The result is a higher-quality protein, i.e., one more usable by your body. These, of course, are not all the possible complementary protein combinations but only those which have been scientifically tested—mostly by nutritionists seeking low-cost protein mixes to cure human protein malnutrition.

First I have included a summary of the complementary protein relationships, Chart X, page 124. Following this chart you'll find twenty different combinations of foods—each accompanied by several recipes. Hopefully the recipes will suggest to you the wide range of possibilities these combinations offer. If you've only thought

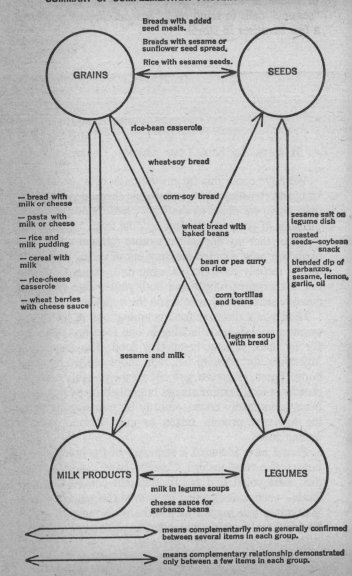

CHART X
SUMMARY OF COMPLEMENTARY PROTEIN RELATIONSHIPS

GRAINS

SEEDS

MILK PRODUCTS

LEGUMES

Breads with added
seed meals.

Breads with sesame or
sunflower seed spread.

Rice with sesame seeds.

rice-bean casserole

wheat-soy bread

corn-soy bread

wheat bread with
baked beans

bean or pea curry
on rice

corn tortillas
and beans

legume soup
with bread

sesame and milk

— bread with
milk or cheese

— pasta with milk or cheese

— rice and
milk pudding

— cereal with
milk

— rice-cheese
casserole

— wheat berries
with cheese sauce

sesame salt on
legume dish

roasted
seeds—soybean
snack

blended dip of
garbanzos,
sesame, lemon,
garlic, oil

milk in legume soups

cheese sauce for
garbanzo beans

means complementarily more generally confirmed
between several items in each group.

means complementary relationship demonstrated
only between a few items in each group.

of beans in terms of pork 'n beans or if the word "sesame" calls to mind only "Sesame Street," you have a few surprises in store!

I. Meat Equivalency Comparisons

Each of the combinations begins with a graphic illustration of the value of eating these particular foods in the same meal rather than in widely separated meals or on different days. For example, eating beans and rice together means that about 43 percent more protein is available to your body than if you use them separately. (Recall that this is true because all the essential amino acids must be present in the correct proportion *simultaneously*.) The advantage thus gained is shown for each combination by first converting the foods, if eaten *separately*, into their protein equivalent as meat and then comparing this amount with the meat equivalent of the foods if eaten *together*. The difference is striking—equal to 1 to 8 ounces of steak!

In the meat equivalency comparisons these differences are also indicated by a figure which gives the percent increase in usable protein. The increase in usable protein is a rough estimate based in most cases on the improved ability of these food combinations to promote growth in experimental animals in contrast to the same foods fed separately. You can refer to Appendix D to see how these estimates were made.

One reason for choosing this technique is to help erase the idea that animal protein is basically different from, and can't therefore be equated with, plant protein. You will remember from the discussion in Part II that this is not true. Based on the ability to stimulate growth in experimental animals, the protein quality of most of the food combinations presented here is equal to or, in many cases, superior to that of meat.

The steak equivalency comparisons serve one additional and important purpose. They show the recommended *proportions* of the foods in each combination—the proportions that, when tested by scientists, provided the greatest amount of usable protein. It is not surprising that the proportions are critical when we recall that the usability of the protein by our bodies depends on the presence of the correct proportions of the essential amino acids.

You may notice that in some cases the proportions of ingredients in the recipes vary from the "ideal proportions" given for that combination. What difference does this make? The answer depends on what type of food protein is increased out of proportion—whether it is a high-quality protein like that of milk or a low-quality protein like that of beans. In the recipes here variations from the proportions given are almost always of the first type—that is, food combinations with a disproportionately large amount of high-quality protein. This is fine. In such a case a *portion* of that total high-quality protein is available in the body to fill the deficiencies in the amino acid pattern of the low-quality protein with which it is combined (such as when a small amount of milk protein complements a much larger amount of protein in wheat). But the remainder of the milk protein is still available to the body at the level of its own quality, which is very high indeed (second only to egg protein). High-quality protein like that in milk products need not obey these proportions because it can, so to speak, stand on its own two feet! The main value of the suggested proportions in such cases is to show you the *minimum* amount of high-quality protein necessary to raise the level of the lower-quality protein with which it is matched.

But what happens in the second case—where a lower-quality protein like that in beans is present in a disproportionately large amount? This is different. It means that the bean protein present above the level that can be complemented (i.e., improved) by the protein in the other food (or foods) in the combination can be used by the body only on the basis of its own quality which is very low. For most beans this would mean that less than half of the protein in that "extra" portion could be used by the body. In these recipes this is exactly what I've tried to avoid. Whenever a dish necessitated more of a low-quality protein than allowed for by the recommended proportions, the recipe was adjusted so that the "extra" low-quality protein was also complemented by another ingredient in the dish (often with a surprising taste improvement too!).

This is quite simple indeed in the many cases where one food protein can be complemented by the protein in several different foods. For example, if I wanted to include more beans in my recipe than the rice-beans proportions allowed, I simply reworked the recipe so that it would taste good, maybe even better, with another protein added that could complement the excess bean protein (sesame or milk, for example).

Thus, the meat equivalency comparisons are designed to illustrate the advantage to be gained by combining certain foods and the recommended proportions to guide you in your own creative cooking. As you read them, don't be distracted by the question of protein *quantity*. If you calculate that the amount of plant protein that one person could eat would equal only a small amount of steak, do not be dismayed. Your idea of a "small amount" of meat might change if you recall from Table VIII in Part III, Section 1, that only 7 ounces of meat could fill your entire day's protein allowance!

The question of protein quantity is handled quite separately. In the beginning of each recipe you will find the estimated grams of usable protein in an average serving of the recipe as well as the percentage of your daily protein allowance that this serving would fill. Since protein allowances are based on body weight, it was necessary to give a range of percents. The percents given cover body weights from 128 to 154 pounds, or the average weights of an American female and male, respectively.

Hopefully the recipes here will just be the first step for you. As you begin wanting to invent your own "complementary protein recipes," you may seek other cookbooks for ideas. At the end of the book, I've included a list of cookbooks that I have found useful.

2. ". . . But it takes too much time"

You may be feeling that cooking in this new way will require too much of your time. After all there are no prepackaged, instant complementary protein combinations on the grocery shelf! I used to resist making even so-called "quick" breads from scratch. How could they be as quick as a ready-made mix? But I began to want to make dishes that demanded I start from scratch. I decided to test myself. How much more time did it actually take to make my cornbread recipe (page 203) than a commercial cornbread mix? I was surprised to find that it hardly took any more time at all! *Both* required that I get out bowls and utensils, mix the batter, oil the baking pan, pour the batter, put it in the oven, clean the mixing utensils, and then the baking pan. The only difference was that for my recipe I had to combine a few more ingredients—a really minor part of the whole operation.

In time I discovered a few tips that make cooking with plant foods quicker, easier, and potentially more creative:

a. Kitchen setup: If all your basic ingredients (grains, flours, dry legumes, nuts, and seeds) are kept in tightly covered jars within reach of the counter (or best of all, *on* the counter) where you work, how easy it is to mix, match (proteins!), and experiment with new combinations.

b. Utensils

(1) *For measuring:* Instead of one large measuring cup, use the type that comes in a set with a different size cup for each fraction. If they have handles, you can use them to scoop the flour, beans, etc., out of your storage jars. Scooping and measuring can then become one step instead of two.

(2) *For chopping:* Cooking with vegetables does require a lot of chopping. If you, like I, are not quite as adept with a knife as Julia Child, you may want to buy a hand vegetable chopper. They cost a couple of dollars but can chop an onion in a flash.

(3) *For blending:* A blender opens up so many interesting cooking possibilities and saves so much time that, if you can afford one, they are great to have. Note that the one- or two-speed blenders are as useful in every way as the very costly ones with many speeds.

(4) *For cooking:* A pressure cooker is also a great aid in cooking just about anything—beans, grains, soups, vegetables, or pudding. Cooking time is two or three times shorter with a pressure cooker. (You can often find very good secondhand ones.)

c. Cooking Habits: Using more plant foods may also require a change in cooking habits. For example, you may not want to take the time to cook a new batch of soybeans every time you want to use them. One answer is to cook legumes, like soybeans, in large batches. You can freeze a portion of the cooked beans to be used later or use them in any of these ways to be eaten immediately, frozen, or refrigerated:

—combined with other ingredients in a casserole or soup;
—pureed and combined with nut butters and seasoning to make a sandwich spread that keeps a very long time in the refrigerator;
—pureed and mixed into a loaf, croquettes, or soup; or
—roasted with seasoning to be eaten like nuts as a snack.

Likewise nuts, seeds, and seed meal can be roasted or made into butters in quite large batches that keep well for a long time in tightly covered jars or in the refrigerator.

Before encouraging you to peruse the recipes for dishes that appeal to you, let me offer one friendly caveat as my final word. The notion of suddenly changing lifelong habits of any kind on the basis of new understanding does not strike me as very realistic or even desirable (however great the revelation!). At least this is not the way it has worked in my family. The change went something like this: The more we learned about the "costliness" of meat on so many grounds and the more we discovered the delicious possibilities of foods we had always neglected, the less important meat became, and eventually the less attractive. Never did we swear off meat, vowing to make this a great sacrifice for the sake of mankind! Rather meat began to play a smaller and smaller role in our diet as it was displaced by new and, frankly, more interesting ways of meeting our daily protein need.

Complementary
Protein Recipes*

*   *   *

---

* Unless stated otherwise, all the ingredients are raw, un-
cooked.

I. Rice and Legumes

Complementary Proportions†

1 cup beans   2⅔ cups rice

Meat Equivalency Comparisons	
	Usable Protein
A. If eaten separately:	*Equivalent to:*
1½ cups beans (or peas)	6¼ oz steak
4 cups rice	7 oz steak
	13¼ oz steak
B. If eaten together: 43% increase	
1½ cups beans (or peas) + 4 cups rice	19 oz steak

You'll find rice in a large number of these combinations and recipes. However, because the amino acid patterns of grains are similar, the substitution of another grain (oatmeal, wheat, rye, barley, etc.) for rice in the combination would probably result in similar complementary effects. Rice is specified here only because it was used in the nutritional tests on which these combinations are based. Rice was chosen for these tests undoubtedly because it is a staple in so many developing countries.

---

† Soybeans are treated separately as combination 2 (140–46).

Feijoada Brazilian Dinner
(Tangy Black Beans–Rice with Sauce–Steamed Greens)

6 servings

Average serving = approx. 11 g usable protein
26 to 31% of daily protein allowance

Beans:

1 cup dry black beans	1 bay leaf
3 cups stock or water (or substitute wine for up to half of stock)	1/4 tsp pepper
	1 orange, whole or halved
	1/2 tsp salt
1 large onion, chopped	2 stalks celery, chopped
2 cloves garlic, chopped	1 tomato, chopped

Sauté the onion and garlic in a little oil, then add them to the beans, with stock, the bay leaf, and pepper. Bring to a boil, simmer 2 minutes, and let sit, covered, for 1 hour. Add the whole or halved orange (whole is the traditional way), salt, celery, and tomato. Simmer, covered with lid ajar, for 2 to 3 hours or more, until the beans are tender. Remove a ladleful of beans, mash them, and return them to the pot to cook until the mashed beans thicken the mixture.

Rice:

2 cups raw brown rice, cooked	2 tbsp butter
1 onion, chopped	2 tomatoes, peeled, seeded, coarsely chopped
3 cloves garlic, minced	
2 tbsp olive oil	

Sauté the onion and garlic in the olive oil and butter until the onion is golden. Add the tomatoes, and simmer a few minutes. Stir in the cooked rice and keep warm over low heat.

Sauces for rice:

1 cup lemon juice
1 small onion
2 cloves garlic
1 peeled and seeded
  tomato

1 tsp green salsa jalapeña,
  or
2 oz canned California
  green chiles, seeded

Blend all ingredients in blender until smooth.

or

1 peeled and seeded
  tomato
California green chiles,
  seeded, to taste
1 tsp salt

2 cloves garlic
juice of one lemon
1 onion, chopped
scallions, parsley, to taste
1/4 cup vinegar

Blend in a blender the first four ingredients until smooth. Stir in the remaining ingredients and, just before serving, stir in a little liquid from the bean pot.

Greens:

1 1/2 lb trimmed greens
  (turnip or mustard greens, collards, etc.)
1 clove minced garlic
1 orange, peeled and sliced
Garnish: 6 heaping tbsp of toasted sesame seed meal*

* Admittedly, sesame seeds are not authentically Brazilian! They are necessary here to complement the "extra" bean protein because this recipe uses more beans than the complementary bean-rice proportions specify.

Steam first three ingredients together until greens are barely wilted. Sprinkle 1 heaping tbsp of toasted seed meal on each serving, with orange slices on top.

Here you have a complete Brazilian dinner. Serve the rice with one of the sauces along with the beans and greens to make a splendid three-course meal.

Roman Rice and Beans

8–10 servings

average serving = approx. 11 g usable protein
26 to 31% of daily protein allowance

1½ cups dried pea beans (cook until tender)
oil as needed
2 large onions, finely chopped
2 garlic cloves, crushed
1–2 carrots, finely chopped
1 stalk celery, chopped (optional)
⅔ cup parsley, chopped
5–6 tsp dried basil
1 tsp dried oregano
2 large tomatoes, coarsely chopped
4–5 tsp salt
pepper to taste
4 cups raw brown rice (cook with 4 tsp salt)
¼–½ cup butter or margarine
1 cup or more grated cheese (Parmesan or jack)

Sauté onions, garlic, carrots, celery, parsley, basil, and oregano in oil until onion is golden. Add tomatoes, salt, pepper, and cooked beans. Add butter and cheese to cooked rice. Then add first mixture. Garnish with more parsley and more grated cheese.

Cream Curry Casserole

6 servings

average serving = approx. 14 g usable protein
32 to 39% of daily protein allowance

2 cups raw brown rice, cooked

¾ cup kidney beans, or small red beans, cooked

2 tbsp butter

1 tbsp arrowroot starch or 2½ tbsp whole wheat flour

2 cups milk

¾ cup instant nonfat dry milk

oil as needed

¼ cup sesame meal

1 medium onion, diced

2 cloves garlic, minced

2 medium carrots, diced

2 small zucchini squash, diced

1 tbsp lemon juice

1 tbsp honey

2 tsp curry powder

1 tsp salt

Mix the rice and beans together and turn into an oiled casserole. Make a cream sauce out of the butter, arrowroot, powdered and liquid milk. Sauté the vegetables and sesame meal until the onion is transparent, adding the zucchini for only the last minute of sautéing. Stir the lemon juice, honey, curry powder, and salt into the cream sauce, then stir in the vegetables. Pour the sauce mixture over the rice and bean mixture. Bake the casserole 20 to 30 minutes at 350°F.

In this recipe the quality of the sesame seed protein is improved by the milk protein.

Oriental Fried Rice

4 servings

average serving = approx. 5 g usable protein
12 to 14% of daily protein allowance

½ cup dry beans, cooked
  with bay leaf
oil as needed
¾ cup onion, chopped
nuts or seeds (optional) ·
1 clove garlic, crushed

1–2 cups more chopped
  vegetables (carrots,
  celery, mushrooms,
  bamboo shoots, etc.)
soy sauce
1⅓ cups raw brown rice,
  cooked (hot if possible)

Oil a *wok* or large frying pan. Place over a medium to high flame and, starting with the onion, sauté the vegetables quickly, just until they are heated through and coated with oil. Do not overcook, as this oriental way of stir-frying vegetables makes a colorful as well as nutritious dish. The quick cooking retains the nutrients in the vegetables better than any other method. Stir the rice into the vegetables and sprinkle with soy sauce (about 1 tbsp). When the rice is hot, stir in the cooked beans (with the bay leaf removed), and serve at once with more soy sauce, with the optional nuts and seeds sprinkled on top.

Masala Dosai
(Indian Filled Pancakes)

6 servings

average serving = approx. 8 g usable protein
19 to 22% of daily protein allowance

I cup raw brown rice	¾ cup sesame meal*
I cup dry yellow split peas	1–2 tsp curry powder
I tsp salt	I small onion, chopped
½–¾ cup buttermilk*	2 tbsp oil

Soak rice and split peas in separate bowls of water overnight. Remove one-third of the split peas and cook until tender. Drain the rice and remaining peas, then grind them together, using water, if necessary, to make a fine paste. Add the salt and whip to make a light batter. Put the mixture in a warm place to ferment for 12 hours. Stir and whip again, adding buttermilk to make a thick or thin batter. (Traditionally the pancakes are made thin.) Brown on both sides on a hot oiled griddle. Place a tablespoon of filling on each pancake, fold all of the pancakes in half, cover the skillet, and steam them for about 1 minute.

Filling: Sauté the onion, sesame meal, and curry powder in the oil until the onion is golden. Puree the peas which have been cooked and blend with the sautéed mixture. If you wish, you may use less sesame meal and serve the pancakes with a yogurt topping.

---

* The sesame protein and the milk protein can both complement the "extra" legume (pea) protein in this recipe.

2. Rice and Soy

Complementary Proportions

¼ cup soybeans or grits	2½ cups rice
or	
½ cup soyflour	
or	
6¼ oz soy curd	

Meat Equivalency Comparisons

	Usable Protein Equivalent to:
A. If eaten separately:	
½ cup soybeans	5 oz steak
5 cups rice	9 oz steak
	⸺
	14 oz steak
B. If eaten together: 32% increase	
½ cup soybeans + 5 cups rice	18½ oz steak

You may wish to eat more soybeans for a given amount of rice than shown in the proportions here. If you do, fine. The "extra" soybean protein will be used by the body according to the quality of soybean protein alone, which is itself fairly high (especially the quality of soy curd protein). You will find that the recipe in this section called "Crusty Soybean Casserole" and the recipes using soy curd (tofu) include considerably more soy protein that these proportions suggest. (Recall that in many cases these recommended proportions are designed to show the *minimum* amount necessary to create a complementary effect.)

Crusty Soybean Casserole

6 servings

average serving = approx. 11 g usable protein
26 to 31% of daily protein allowance

½ cup dry soybeans,
  cooked
2 cups corn, fresh or frozen
2 cups canned tomatoes
1 cup chopped onion
½ cup chopped celery
1 clove crushed garlic
½ tsp each thyme and
  summer savory
2 tsp salt

pinch cayenne
¼ cup tomato paste
3 tbsp brewer's yeast
½ cup stock
wheat germ
⅓ cup grated cheese
butter
2½ cups raw brown rice,
  cooked

Combine soybeans, corn, tomatoes, onion, celery, garlic, herbs, spices, and salt. Combine tomato paste, brewer's yeast, and stock.

Place half of the cooked rice on the bottom of an oiled 4- to 6-quart casserole. Cover with the vegetable mixture. Spread the tomato paste over the vegetables, and cover all with the rest of the rice. Sprinkle with grated cheese and then wheat germ. Dot with butter and bake uncovered for 30 minutes at 350°F.

Stuffed Cabbage Leaves

4 servings

average serving = approx. 9 g usable protein
21 to 25% of daily protein allowance

1¼ cup raw brown rice
  and ⅛ cup soygrits,
  cooked together
1 onion, chopped, sauteed
  in oil as needed
½ cup pignolia nuts (or
  toasted sunflower seeds)
1 scant tbsp caraway seed

¼ cup raisins
½ tsp salt
1 15-oz. can tomato sauce
  (sweetened with 1 tbsp
  brown sugar, if desired)
12 whole cabbage leaves,
  steamed briefly
1 cup yogurt

Mix all, except last three ingredients. Add enough tomato sauce to moisten mixture. Place about 3 tbsp of this mixture on each cabbage leaf and roll up. Secure with a toothpick, if necessary. Place the rolls in a covered skillet and pour the remaining tomato sauce over them. Cook about 15 minutes or until cabbage is tender. The contrast of the green cabbage and the red tomato sauce makes this dish quite beautiful. It is especially good topped with yogurt.

Variations:
1. Moisten mixture with 1 beaten egg instead of the tomato sauce.
2. Instead of removing leaves from the cabbage, cut out the center of the cabbage, boil 10 minutes and then fill with stuffing.

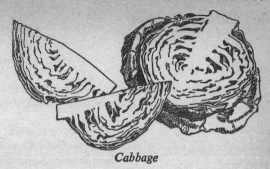

Cabbage

Curry Rice

4 servings

average serving = approx. 8 g usable protein
19 to 22% of daily protein allowance

1 tbsp butter
1 tbsp curry powder
½ cup mixed nuts and
  raisins
1 onion, sliced

1 apple, cored and sliced
1¼ cups raw brown rice
2 tbsp soy grits
3 cups stock or water
yogurt

Brown curry, nuts, onion, and apple in butter. Stir the rice and soy grits into the stock. Add the curry mixture and cook until the rice is tender and all liquid is absorbed. Serve with yogurt.

Variations:
  1. Add 1 tsp coriander seeds.
  2. Omit curry and add 1 cup shredded cabbage and 1 tsp caraway seed.
  3. Omit soy grits and add ½ cup sesame seed.

Leafy Chinese Tofu (Soy Curd)

2 servings

average serving = approx. 19 g usable protein
44 to 53% of daily protein allowance

1¼ cup tofu, cut into 1-inch cubes (½ lb)
oil as needed
spinach or any leafy green vegetable—torn into bite-size pieces

sesame salt, or toasted seed (see Basic Cooking Instructions, Appendix A)
soy sauce
1 cup raw brown rice, cooked

Oil a large frying pan. Sauté tofu cubes about 5 minutes. Push the cubes to the center of the pan and spread the torn spinach all around edge.

Sprinkle the tofu with sesame salt and soy sauce. Cover the pan to steam the spinach until it is just wilted. Be careful not to overcook it. Remove from heat and drain excess liquid. Sprinkle soy sauce over the spinach, and serve with rice.

Variation: Spread a mixture of miso (soybean paste) and sesame butter, blended in equal proportions, on one side of sliced tofu and sprinkle with wheat germ. While you brown this side spread the miso-sesame mixture and sprinkle wheat germ on the second side. Turn once more to brown the second side.

Sukiyaki

4 servings

average serving = approx. 10 g usable protein
23 to 28% of daily protein allowance

1½ cups raw brown rice,
cooked
½ cup thinly sliced onions
4–5 sliced mushrooms
¼ cup soy sauce mixed
with ¾ cup water and a
pinch of sugar
1 bunch Swiss chard, sliced
(or bok choy or spinach)

5–6 leaves Chinese
cabbage, sliced (or 2–3
stalks celery)
¼ cup sliced water
chestnuts
5–6 green onions, chopped
½ cup bean sprouts
8–16 oz tofu

In a heavy skillet sauté onions and mushrooms briefly
in a little oil. Add a few teaspoons of the soy sauce
mixture and the Chinese cabbage or celery. Add more
liquid and the Swiss chard, water chestnuts, and green
onions. Cook these 5 minutes adding liquid as needed.
Add the sprouts and tofu, cooking long enough to heat
them both thoroughly. Serve over rice.

Traditionally this dish is cooked at table so that the
vegetables can be eaten immediately. The dish can be
made most attractive if you cut the vegetables in large
interesting shapes.

3. Rice and Wheat and Soy

Complementary Proportions

1 cup rice	1 cup whole wheat flour	1 cup soy flour
	or	**or**
	¾ cup bulgur wheat	⅔ cup soybeans or grits
		.19 oz soy curd (tofu)

Meat Equivalency Comparisons

	Usable Protein Equivalent to:
A. If eaten separately:	
1 cup rice	1¾ oz steak
¾ cup bulgur wheat (or 1 cup wheat flour)	1¼ oz steak
⅔ cup soybeans	6½ oz steak
	9½ oz steak
B. If eaten together: 24% increase	
1 cup rice + ¾ cup bulgur wheat + ⅔ cup soybeans	11¾ oz steak

Celery, Onion, Lemon, Garlic, Kidney Bean, Chick Pea

Hearty Vegetable Soup

about 3 quarts

1 cup⌐= approx. 3 g usable protein
7 to 8% of daily protein allowance

⅓ cup dry soybeans,
  cooked with bay leaf
2 tbsp olive oil
1 cup onions, chopped
2 cups vegetables,
  chopped (carrots, mush-
  rooms, celery, etc.)
1 cup canned tomatoes
  (drain and reserve liquid)
2–3 peppercorns
pinch cayenne
2 tbsp nutritional yeast
½ tsp each basil, tarragon,
  oregano, celery seed,
  summer savory

¼ tsp each thyme, rose-
  mary, marjoram, sage
2 tbsp soy sauce
½ cup raw brown rice
⅓–½ cup raw bulgur
  wheat, or ⅓ cup raw
  whole wheat kernels
1 heaping tbsp miso (soy
  paste)
6–8 cups vegetable stock,
  including liquid from
  tomatoes

Sauté onions and chopped vegetables briefly in olive oil. Add the tomatoes, the herbs and spices, soy sauce, grains, cooked soybeans, and the stock. Bring the soup to a boil. Remove about ½ cup of liquid to a small bowl. Add the miso to the hot liquid and mix thoroughly until you have a thin, soft paste. Add the paste back to the soup. Simmer for 1–2 hours until the grains are tender *or* pressure cook 10–15 minutes.

This soup gets heartier each time you reheat it. It makes a full meal with bread and cheese.

Sweet and Pungent Vegetable Curry

8 servings

average serving = approx. 15 g usable protein
35 to 42% of daily protein allowance

1 1/3 cup soybeans, cooked with about 2 cups extra water
2 cups raw brown rice and 1 1/2 cups raw bulgur—cooked together
5 carrots, sliced thickly
2–3 onions, sliced thinly
1/4 cup flour
1 tbsp (or more) hot curry powder
1 cup (or more) raisins
1 cup raw cashews
3 tbsp (or more) mango chutney
1 tbsp raw sugar

Sauté onions and carrots in small amount of oil. Add curry powder and flour; cook 1 minute. Stir in liquid from beans (at least 1 cup). Simmer until carrots are tender but not soft. Add remaining ingredients and more liquid if necessary. Adjust seasoning. Simmer until raisins are soft and seasonings mingle. Serve on the grains. A delightful combination—perfect for the most festive occasion.

Mexican Grains

8 servings

average serving = approx. 7 g usable protein
16 to 20% of daily protein allowance

1 cup raw brown rice plus ¾ cup raw bulgur, cooked together	½ lb string beans, sliced into 2-inch pieces
⅔ cup dry soybeans, cooked	1 tsp chili powder (to taste)
oil as needed	dash hot sauce
2 tbsp green chilis, diced	salt and pepper
	1 16-oz can stewed tomatoes
	1 small can corn

Heat oil in heavy pot or skillet. Add the green chilis and sauté until tender. To the chilis add the sliced string beans and continue sautéing while adding in the chili powder, hot sauce, and salt and pepper. Mix in the stewed tomatoes, corn, grains, and soybeans. Simmer for about 15 minutes.

Variation: Cook the vegetables as directed, but do not stir in the grains. Serve the vegetables over the grains instead.

Rice-Wheat "Kasha"

5 servings

average serving = approx. 15 g usable protein
35 to 42% of daily protein allowance

1 cup raw brown rice	3 eggs, beaten
¾ cup bulgur wheat	1 quart stock, boiling
⅔ cup soy grits	½ cup butter

Toast grains and soy grits in a dry pan on top of stove, stirring often (or toast in a 250°F oven on a cookie sheet). When the mixture is cool, spread it on the bottom of a cold heavy skillet. Add eggs one at a time, stirring to coat every grain. Put the pan over medium heat and cook the grains until they're dry, stirring constantly to break up lumps. Add the boiling stock and butter. Cover and simmer until the grains are tender. Goes beautifully with steamed greens, or a sweet and sour steamed cabbage dish.

4. Rice and Yeast

Complementary Proportions

I cup rice   ¼ cup brewer's yeast (4 tbsp)

Meat Equivalency Comparisons	
	Usable Protein
A. If eaten separately:	*Equivalent to:*
½ cup brewer's yeast	3½ oz steak
2 cups rice	3½ oz steak
	———
	⎰ 7 oz steak
B. If eaten together: 57% increase	⎱
½ cup brewer's yeast + 2 cups rice	11 oz steak

Rice and yeast makes an especially "potent" combination. In these proportions the mix is able to stimulate growth in experimental animals at a rate almost equal to milk.

The taste of different types of brewer's yeast varies enormously. Some types add a nutty flavor to a recipe; others, if used in too great a quantity, can detract from the dish. If you find that 4 tablespoons of your brewer's yeast per cup of raw rice is too much, you can substitute sesame seed or nonfat dried milk for part of the yeast.

Mediterranean Lemon Soup

6 servings

one serving = 6 g usable protein
14 to 17% of daily protein allowance

1½ quarts of vegetable
  stock (saved from cook-
  ing vegetables or beans)
½ cup raw brown rice
salt, if necessary
¼ tsp summer savory

2 tbsp brewer's yeast
4 eggs, beaten
juice and grated rind of
  1–2 lemons (you can
  start with the lesser
  amount and add more to
  taste at the end)

Heat stock to boiling and stir in rice and salt. Cover and simmer about 30 minutes. Mix savory and yeast into eggs. Add lemon juice and rind and mix again. Take 1 cup of hot stock and slowly add it to the egg mixture. Stir constantly. Remove stock from heat and gradually add egg mixture to it. Serve.

The clean, fresh taste of this soup makes a perfect beginning to many different types of meals. We have enjoyed it with the Middle Eastern Tacos (in combination 14), with fish entrées, and with many vegetable casseroles.

Savory Rice

3 servings

average serving = approx. 8 g usable protein
19 to 22% of daily protein allowance

oil as needed
1/2 cup celery, chopped
1/2 cup onions, chopped
1/2 cup green pepper,
    chopped
1/2 cup carrots, chopped
1 clove garlic, crushed

1/4 tsp each paprika, sage,
    marjoram, and rosemary
2 cups stock, hot
1/2 tsp salt
4 tbsp brewer's yeast*
1 cup raw brown rice

Sauté all of the vegetables in the oil until the onions
are golden and the celery is tender. Stir in the herbs to
coat them with oil. Add the stock and bring the mixture
to a boil. Add the rice and stir in the salt and brewer's
yeast. Lower the heat, cover and simmer until the rice
has absorbed all of the liquid.

You can vary the vegetables and the herbs in this
recipe, using whatever you have available, or any favorite combinations.

---

* Depending on the taste of your brewer's yeast, you may
wish to substitute toasted sesame seed for part of the yeast.

Cold Gallentine

6 servings

serving = approx. 6 g usable protein
14 to 17% of daily protein allowance

2 tbsp butter
1 medium onion, chopped
1/4 pound mushrooms,
    coarsely chopped
2 eggs, beaten
1 tsp salt
pepper to taste

pinch nutmeg
1/2 cup raw brown rice,
    cooked
2 tbsp brewer's yeast*
3/4 cup bread crumbs
1/4 cup nuts, ground

Brown onion and mushrooms in butter. Beat the spices and salt into the eggs. Combine the rest of the ingredients, add the eggs, mushrooms, and onions. Place the mixture in an oiled casserole. Bake at 375°F for 1 hour. Serve cold with a spread made of:

2 tbsp ricotta cheese
2 tbsp yogurt
2 tbsp mayonnaise

Makes a fine hors d'oeuvre or lunchtime dish.

Variation: 2 or 3 whole or halved hard boiled eggs can be placed in center of mixture before baking.

---

* Depending on the taste of your brewer's yeast, you may wish to substitute toasted sesame seed for part of the yeast.

5. Rice and Sesame Seeds

Complementary Proportions

1 cup rice	1/3 cup sesame seed
	or
	1/2 cup sesame meal
	or
	3 tbsp sesame butter

Meat Equivalency Comparisons		Usable Protein Equivalent to:
A. If eaten separately:		
1 cup sesame seed (or 1 1/2 cups seed meal)		3 oz steak
3 cups rice		5 1/4 oz steak
		‾‾‾‾‾‾‾‾
		8 1/4 oz steak
B. If eaten together:	21% increase	
1 cup sesame seed + 3 cups rice		10 oz steak

Throughout the complementary combinations you'll find that sesame seed is frequently included while sunflower seed is hardly ever mentioned. You shouldn't be misled to think that this means sesame seeds are necessarily superior. As far as I can tell they just happened to be chosen for the experiments to determine complementarity. You may remember from the protein tables that sunflower seeds actually contain more protein and have a slightly higher NPU score. Since their amino acid patterns are very similiar, you could probably substitute sunflower seed when sesame is called for and the same complementary effects would still hold true.

Tangy Rice-Sesame Pudding

6 servings

average serving = approx. 6 g usable protein
14 to 17% of daily protein allowance

¾ cup raw brown rice,
  cooked
2–2½ cups orange juice
6 tbsp sesame meal
⅔ cup brown sugar,
  packed
grated rind of one orange
  (can use blender)

4 eggs, well beaten
½ tsp each cinnamon and
  ginger
¼ tsp nutmeg
1 tsp vanilla extract
½ cup raisins (optional)

Combine all the ingredients well. Place in oiled baking dish and bake at 350°F for 1 hour, or until firm. Especially good served warm.

Sesame Eggplant Parmesan

6 servings

average serving = approx. 12 g usable protein
28 to 34% of daily protein allowance

1 large or 2 medium egg-
  plants, sliced ½ inch
  thick
oil as needed
2 cups canned tomatoes (1
  28-oz can, mostly
  drained)
½ tsp salt
1 tbsp chopped parsley
1 bay leaf
¼ tsp oregano
¼ tsp thyme
¼ tsp rosemary

2 cloves garlic, crushed
2 tbsp onion, grated
2 tbsp green pepper,
  grated
2 tbsp grated carrot
½ cup Parmesan cheese,
  grated
1 cup sesame meal, toasted
½ pound mozzarella
  cheese, sliced thinly
2 cups raw brown rice,
  cooked

Sauté the eggplant slices in oil over high heat until browned slightly, drain on paper towels, and set aside. Combine tomatoes, seasonings, and grated vegetables in a skillet, cover, and simmer 15 minutes. Remove bay leaf, add Parmesan cheese, sesame seed meal, and blend well. Place a layer of eggplant in an oiled, shallow 2-quart baking dish. Cover with half the tomato sauce, then half the mozzarella cheese. Repeat layers, and bake at 350°F about 30 minutes, until cheese is melted and begins to brown. Serve over the cooked rice.

Confetti Rice

4 servings

average serving = approx. 7 g usable protein
16 to 20% of daily protein allowance

1 cup raw brown rice,
  cooked
oil as needed
1 small onion, chopped
1 cup mixed dried fruits,
  chopped

⅔ cup mixed nuts,*
  chopped
⅓ cup sesame seeds or ½
  cup seed meal
¼–½ tsp cloves
½ tsp salt
4 tbsp melted butter

In hot oil, sauté onion, mixed fruit, nuts, and sesame
seed or meal until the onion is golden. Stir in the cloves
and salt, and then mix with the cooked rice. Place in a
small casserole. Pour the melted butter over all. Bake
15–20 minutes at 350°F.

---

* If you used peanuts and added sunflower seeds, to complement their protein, you would probably have lots more usable
protein.

Sesame-Rice Fritter-Puffs

4 servings

average serving = approx. 7 g usable protein
16 to 20% of daily protein allowance

⅔ cup raw brown rice,
   cooked
1 tsp salt
¼ cup sesame seeds
¼ cup milk

2 eggs, separated
2 tbsp whole wheat flour
⅛ tsp pepper
vegetable oil for frying

Toast sesame seeds until golden. Mix milk, egg yolks, flour and pepper, and salt if needed. Combine milk mixture, sesame seeds, and rice; mix well. Fold in stiffly beaten egg whites. Drop by tablespoonfuls onto hot oiled griddle and fry until brown. Drain on absorbent paper.

Good with curry sauce or cream sauce.

Sesame Vegetable Rice

2 servings

average serving = approx. 5 g usable protein
12 to 14% of daily protein allowance

⅔ cup raw brown rice, cooked
oil as needed
thin sliced mixed vegetables: carrots, celery, onion,
    broccoli, squash, cabbage, garlic, etc.
¼ cup toasted sesame seeds
soy sauce

Sauté the vegetables in a minimum of oil beginning with those that take the longest to cook. The vegetables should be crisp and heated through. Be careful not to overcook them. Serve the vegetables on cooked rice and sprinkle with sesame seeds. Pour soy sauce over all.

Squash

Fruit Pancakes

6 servings

average serving = approx. 8 g usable protein
19 to 22% of daily protein allowance

1 cup whole wheat flour	3 eggs, separated
1/3 cup sesame seed meal	1 1/2 cups milk (or more for a thin batter)
1 tbsp baking powder	
1 tbsp brown sugar	1/4 cup oil
1/2 tsp salt	1 cup fruit chunks (apples, pears, peaches, bananas, berries, etc.)
3/4 cup raw brown rice, cooked	

Stir together the flour, seed meal, baking powder, sugar, and salt. Beat the egg yolks, blend in the milk and oil, then stir in the rice, blending it well so there are no big lumps of grain. Stir the wet ingredients into the dry, using the fewest strokes possible. Just be sure the dry ingredients are wet. Fold in the egg whites that have been beaten until stiff. Then gently fold in the fruit. Bake on a hot, oiled griddle.

6. Rice and Milk

Complementary Proportions

¾ cup rice	1 cup skim milk
	or
	3½ tbsp nonfat dry milk
	or
	5 tbsp instant nonfat dry milk
	or
	about 1¼ oz cheese, ¼ cup grated

Meat Equivalency Comparisons	
	Usable Protein
A. If eaten separately:	**Equivalent to:**
1½ cup rice	2⅔ oz steak
2 cups skim milk	3⅓ oz steak
	6 oz steak
B. If eaten together: 29% increase	
1½ cups rice + 2 cups skim milk	7¾ oz steak

You will notice that I have translated the milk protein proportion into its cheese equivalent. Although the cheese was not actually tested, based on the similarity of the amino acid patterns of milk and cheese, one could assume that cheese can also complement rice. This assumption is confirmed by recalling a parallel case: that is, we know that both milk *and* cheese can complement wheat protein.

Parmesan Rice

2 servings

average serving = approx. 10 g usable protein
23 to 28% of daily protein allowance

⅔ cup raw brown rice, cooked with 1 tsp salt
2 tbsp butter, melted
1 egg, beaten

¼ cup grated Parmesan cheese
juice of 1 lemon
pepper to taste

Stir the melted butter into the cooked rice. Mix the grated cheese, lemon juice, and pepper into the beaten egg, and then blend with the rice. Simmer 5 minutes and serve immediately.

This goes well with cooked zucchini or eggplant. It can be easily multiplied.

Rice Cream and Sesame Cereal

4 servings

average serving = approx. 10 g usable protein
23 to 28% of daily protein allowance

To make rice cream powder:

Grind raw brown rice that has been washed in a blender until it is very fine, *or*:

For a nuttier cereal, roast the washed rice in a dry pan over medium heat until it is well browned. Grind in the blender (the roasted rice will grind more finely than the raw rice, above). Then roast the powder again in a dry pan. Store the cooled powder in a tightly covered container.

To prepare the cereal:

4 cups milk
2 tsp salt
1 cup rice cream
  powder (ground from ¾
  cup raw rice)

1 tbsp brewer's yeast
2 tbsp sesame seed meal,
  raw or roasted

Bring milk and salt to boiling point, add rice cream powder, stirring constantly. Lower heat and simmer, covered, about 10 minutes, or until cereal is thick. Stir in sesame meal and brewer's yeast.

Serve with more roasted sesame meal, milk, butter, honey, or molasses. Try making the cereal with wheat, rye, or corn flour and sunflower seeds.

Con Queso Rice

6 servings

average serving = approx. 17 g usable protein
39 to 47% of daily protein allowance

1½ cups raw brown rice (cooked with salt and pepper)
¾ lb shredded jack cheese
1 small can chiles, chopped
½ lb ricotta cheese thinned slightly with milk or yogurt

3 cloves garlic, minced or pressed
½ cup grated cheddar
1 large onion, chopped
½ cup dry black beans (or blackeyed peas), cooked

Mix rice, beans, garlic, onion, chiles. Layer this mixture alternately in a greased casserole with jack cheese and ricotta (spreading evenly over casserole). End with rice mixture. Bake at 350°F for ½ hour. During last few minutes of baking, sprinkle grated cheese over the top.

This is an ideal dish for a buffet dinner. My guests always ask for this recipe!

Cream of Tomato and Rice Soup

6 servings

average serving = approx. 5 g usable protein
12 to 14% of daily protein allowance

7 fresh tomatoes quartered, or the equivalent canned
1 carrot, chopped
1 onion, chopped
1/2 cup celery, chopped
1 clove garlic, minced
oil as needed
2 tbsp whole wheat flour

1 tsp salt
4 white peppercorns
1 tbsp sugar
1 tsp each oregano, basil
3/4 cup raw rice, cooked
3 cups vegetable stock or water
3 cups milk

Sauté carrot, onion, and celery, until onion is golden. Add flour and mix. Add stock, tomatoes, garlic, salt, peppercorns, sugar, and herbs. Simmer for an hour— or at least long enough for the flavors to mingle. Puree through a sieve or in a blender. Return to pan and add rice and milk. Reheat slowly (but don't boil) and serve immediately with crisp croutons. Hmmm, good.

If you don't wish to take the time to make this soup "as the French make it," merely delete the sauté step, blend ingredients in a blender, add the rice, and simmer for as long as you can. Add the milk. Serve.

Spinach Casserole

4 servings

average serving = approx. 10 g usable protein
23 to 28% of daily protein allowance

¾ cup raw brown rice,
  cooked
½ cup grated cheddar
  cheese
1 lb fresh spinach, chopped
2 eggs, beaten

2 tbsp parsley, chopped
½ tsp salt
¼ tsp pepper
2 tbsp wheat germ
1 tbsp butter, melted

Combine the cooked rice and cheese. Combine the
eggs, parsley, salt, and pepper. Add the two mixtures together and stir in the raw spinach. Pour into an oiled
casserole. Top with wheat germ which has been mixed
with the melted butter. Bake in a 350°F oven for 35
minutes.

Serve this casserole with a contrasting vegetable such
as sautéed carrots or yellow squash and hot Pineapple-
Corn Muffins. A light, delicious meal.

Walnut-Cheddar Loaf

4 servings

average serving = approx. 13 g usable protein
30 to 36% of daily protein allowance

1 cup black walnuts,
  ground (can use blender)
1 cup cheese, grated
1/2 cup raw brown rice,
  cooked

2 cups chopped onions,
  sautéed
2 eggs, beaten
1/4 tsp salt
2 tbsp nutritional yeast
1 tsp caraway seeds

Combine all ingredients. Place in oiled loaf pan. Bake at 350°F for 30 minutes.

Especially nice if served with a cheese sauce with whole walnuts sprinkled on top.

7. Wheat Products with Milk or Cheese

Complementary Proportions

1 cup milk **or** 1⅓ oz cheese	:	5 slices bread **or** 1 cup dry macaroni

or

1 cup whole wheat flour	:	2 tbsp nonfat dry milk (3½ instant) **or** slightly more than ½ cup skim milk

---

Meat Equivalency Comparisons

	Usable Protein Equivalent to:
With Milk	
A. If eaten separately:	
3 cups whole wheat flour	5 oz steak
6 tbsp nonfat dry milk	
(slightly more than ⅓ cup)	3 oz steak
	⎯
	⎧ 8 oz steak
B. If eaten together: 13% increase	⎨
3 cups whole wheat flour + 6 tbsp	
nonfat dry milk	⎩ 9 oz steak
With Cheese	
A. If eaten separately:	
1 oz cheese	1 oz steak
4 slices whole wheat bread	
(or ¾ cup dry macaroni)	1 oz steak
	⎯
	⎧ 2 oz steak
B. If eaten together: 25% increase	⎨
1 oz cheese + 4 slices whole wheat bread	⎩ 2½ oz steak

This combination was cited in the introduction as a case where a high-quality protein complements a lower-quality protein. Here, you will recall, the proportions indicate the minimal amount of animal protein (milk) necessary to increase the usability of the wheat protein. Because most of us are fortunate enough to be able to afford more of the milk protein and thus more total protein, the following recipes include much more of certain milk products than is indicated by these complementary proportions.

Noodle Cheese Soufflé

6–8 servings

average serving = approx. 14 g usable protein
32 to 39% of daily protein allowance

3 eggs, separated
1/4 cup butter, melted
2 tbsp honey
1 lb partially creamed cottage cheese (about 2 cups)
1 cup yogurt

1/2 lb whole wheat or wheat-soy noodles, cooked
1/2 cup whole grain bread crumbs
butter as needed

Beat the egg yolks, add the melted butter, honey, cottage cheese, yogurt, and then the cooked noodles. Beat the egg whites until stiff and fold carefully into the noodle mixture. Pour into a 2-quart oiled casserole. Top with bread crumbs and dot with butter. Bake at 375°F for 45 minutes.

This is a delicious and elegant dish which you can vary by adding 1/2 to 1 cup of raisins before the addition of the noodles.

Macaroni Salad Ricotta

4 servings

average serving = approx. 7 g usable protein
16 to 20% of daily protein allowance

1/4 lb whole wheat maca-
roni, cooked tender,
drained and chilled
1 cup ricotta cheese, mixed
with 2 tsp mustard and
thinned with yogurt so
that it will mix in the
salad like mayonnaise
1/4 cup sliced or chopped
ripe olives

1 bell pepper, chopped
coarsely
2 scallions and tops
chopped
1 tbsp chopped parsley
red pimentoes, to taste
1/2 tsp each, dill and basil
salt and pepper, to taste

Mix all ingredients and serve on a bed of lettuce.
Colorful, light, and satisfying.

Wine, Bread, Cheese and Thou

about 6 open sandwiches

one sandwich = approx. 6 g usable protein
14 to 17% of daily protein allowance

4 tbsp butter	1 cup cheese, diced
4 tbsp whole wheat flour	bread—stale is preferable
1 cup milk, hot	—about 6 slices
salt and pepper	wine as needed
1 egg yolk, beaten	

Melt the butter, add flour and blend well. Stir in milk, salt, and pepper. Cook over low heat until the mixture is very thick. Remove from heat and stir in the egg yolk and cheese. Dip each piece of bread quickly into the wine, or sprinkle the wine over the bread. Be careful to not let the bread get soggy. Put the slices on an oiled baking sheet, spread with the cheese mixture and bake at 400°F for 10 minutes, until slightly puffed and browned.

Variation: Add ½ cup of minced onions to the cheese sauce mixture.

Ricotta Lasagne Swirls

4 servings

average serving = approx. 14 g usable protein
32 to 39% of daily protein allowance

8 cooked lasagne noodles

Filling:
2 bunches spinach, finely
   chopped
2 tbsp Parmesan cheese
1 cup ricotta cheese (1/2 lb)
1/4 tsp nutmeg
salt and pepper to taste

Sauce:
2 cups tomato sauce
2 cloves garlic, minced and
   sautéed
1/2 cup onions, chopped
   and sautéed
1/2 tsp basil
salt and pepper to taste

Steam spinach until it is quite limp, but not mushy.
You don't need any water to do this. Just put the washed
spinach in a pan which has a tight-fitting lid and cook
it over low heat about 7 minutes. Mix the spinach with
the cheeses, nutmeg, salt, and pepper. Coat each noodle
with 2 to 3 tbsp of the mixture along its entire length,
roll up, turn on end so that you see the spiral, and place
in a shallow baking pan. Mix all of the sauce ingredients
together and pour over all rolled-up noodles. Bake at
350°F for 20 minutes. (You can substitute your favorite
tomato sauce recipe or use the pizza sauce in combination 9.)

This is an especially attractive dish and much lighter
than most Italian-style pasta dishes.

Variation: Use part of the spinach in the filling and
part in the sauce.

Easy and Elegant Cheese Soufflé

5 servings

average serving = approx. 20 g usable protein
46 to 56% of daily protein allowance

3 cups grated cheese
4–6 slices bread
2 cups milk or 1½ cups
  milk and ½ cup liquor
  (wine or vermouth)
3 eggs, beaten

½ tsp salt
½ tsp Worcestershire
  sauce
½ tsp thyme
½ tsp dry mustard
pepper

Layer the cheese and bread in an oiled baking dish, starting with the bread. Pour over it the milk or milk mixture. Beat, with the eggs, the salt and remaining ingredients and pour this over the bread mixture also. Let stand for 30 minutes. Bake at 350°F 1 hour in a pan of hot water.

This dish sounds so very easy and homey, but is truly elegant. When you take it out of the oven, you yourself won't believe how simply it was made. In a deep dish it has the appearance of a soufflé; in a shallow dish it resembles a quiche.

Gourmet Curried Eggs on Toast (or Rice)

4 to 6 servings

average serving = 16 g usable protein
37 to 44% of daily protein allowance

8 large eggs, hard-boiled
2 tbsp margarine
3 tbsp flour
I tbsp curry powder (more
 or less to taste)
1/2 tsp beau monde seasoning (optional)

1/4 cup sherry
2 cups milk
salt and pepper
1/2 cup shredded Swiss
 cheese (or more)
vegetable protein "bacon"
 bits (optional)
4–6 slices toast (or 11/2–2
 cups raw rice, cooked)
chopped parsley (optional)

Melt margarine over low heat (preferably in the top
of a double boiler). Blend in the flour, curry powder,
and sherry. Slowly add milk, then beau monde, salt, and
pepper. Cook 5 minutes, stirring. (Sauce will seem thin
now but it thickens in baking.)

Place eggs, sliced in half, in an oiled casserole. Cover
with curry sauce. Sprinkle with "bacon" bits and shredded cheese. Bake for 20 minutes at 350°F. Serve over
toast (or rice). Sprinkle with chopped parsley if you did
not use the "bacon" bits.

This simple casserole has a truly "gourmet" flavor.
It is especially good served with cooked spinach, asparagus, or broccoli.

8. Wheat and Beans

Complementary Proportions

½ cup beans   2½ cups bulgur wheat
or
3 cups whole wheat flour

Meat Equivalency Comparisons	
A. If eaten separately:	**Usable Protein Equivalent to:**
½ cup beans	2 oz steak
3 cups whole wheat flour	5 oz steak
	‾
	7 oz steak
B. If eaten together: 33% increase	9⅓ oz steak
½ cup beans + 3 cups whole wheat flour	

Tabouli

Zesty Lebanese Salad

6 servings

**average serving = approx. 4 g usable protein
9 to 11% of daily protein allowance**

¼ cup dry white or gar-
   banzo beans, cooked and
   drained
1¼ cups bulgur wheat, raw
4 cups boiling water
1½ cups minced parsley*
¾ cup mint, minced* (if
   not available, substitute
   more parsley)
¾ cup minced scallions

3 medium tomatoes,
   chopped
¾ cup lemon juice
¼ cup olive oil
1–2 tsp salt
freshly ground pepper to
   taste
raw grape, lettuce, or
   cabbage leaves

Pour the boiling water over the bulgur and let stand
about 2 hours until the wheat is light and fluffy. Drain
excess water and shake in a strainer or press with hands
to remove as much water as possible. Mix the bulgur,
cooked beans, and remaining ingredients. Chill for at
least 1 hour. Serve on raw leaves.

This recipe is adapted from a traditional Lebanese
dish often served on festive occasions. If you want to
be truly authentic, let your guests or family scoop it up
with lettuce leaves instead of using spoons. A Lebanese
friend once served Tabouli as a party hors-d'oeuvre.
It was a great hit.

---

* You can use blender. A wooden chopstick is good for scrap-
ing leaves from sides of blender into blade action.

Stuffed Eggplant

4 servings

average serving = approx. 8 g usable protein
19 to 22% of daily protein allowance

1 large onion, minced	½ tsp basil
¼ pound mushrooms, chopped	½ tsp oregano
	1 tbsp parsley, chopped
oil as needed	2 tsp salt
1¼ cups raw bulgur wheat	½ tsp pepper
2½ cups water or stock	1 6-oz can tomato paste
¼ cup dry garbanzo beans, cooked	2 cans water
	salt and pepper
¼ lb fresh peas, shelled	2 eggplants, halved

Sauté the onion in the oil until transparent. Add the mushrooms and sauté until the onion is golden. Stir in the raw bulgur, coating each kernel with oil. Sauté the mixture until the bulgur begins to brown. Add the stock, cover, and cook until the bulgur is tender and all of the liquid is absorbed. Mix the cooked bulgur with the garbanzos, peas, basil, oregano, parsley, salt, and pepper. Remove most of the pulp from the eggplants, leaving a 1-inch-thick shell. Chop the pulp and add it to the bulgur mixture.

Blend the tomato paste with the 2 cans water, add salt and pepper to taste, and oregano and basil if desired. Place eggplant halves in a large oiled casserole. Fill each half with a generous amount of stuffing. Pour the sauce over, cover the casserole, and bake at 325°F for 45 to 60 minutes. During the last half of baking, remove the cover from the casserole, and baste the eggplants if necessary.

This recipe can easily be used for stuffing either green peppers or tomatoes.

Spanish Bulgur

4 servings

average serving = approx. 6 g usable protein
14 to 17% of daily protein allowance

1¼ cups raw bulgur
2 tbsp cooking oil
½ cup chopped green
  onions
½ green pepper, diced
1 No. 2 can tomatoes

¼–½ cup dry beans
  (cooked tender)
1 clove garlic, minced
1 tsp salt
⅛ tsp ground pepper
1 tsp paprika
dash cayenne

Cook and stir bulgur in oil until golden. Add remaining ingredients. Cover, bring to boil, reduce heat, simmer 15 minutes, adding hot water if necessary.

Bulgur and Bean Salad

6 servings

average serving = approx. 4 g usable protein
9 to 11% of daily protein allowance

1¼ cups dry bulgur wheat
2 tbsp oil
2½ cups stock or water
¼ cup dry beans, cooked
   (small kidneys are good)
2 tomatoes, halved and
   sliced

favorite salad vegetables
including:
   lettuce, torn
   spinach, torn
   carrots, sliced
   radishes, sliced
   celery, diced
   zucchini, sliced
   fresh peas, etc.

Sauté the raw bulgur in the oil, stirring until all of the grains are coated and the bulgur is golden. Add the stock which has been heated to boiling, cover tightly, and cook until all the liquid is absorbed and the grains are tender. Refrigerate while you prepare the vegetables for the salad. When the bulgur is cold, stir in the cooked beans and toss with the salad vegetables.

Served with Italian dressing, this salad will make a whole meal with the addition of bread and cheese.

9. Whole Wheat and Soy

Complementary Proportions

1 cup whole wheat flour   1/4 cup soy flour
                                   or
                               1/8 cup soy grits or soybeans
                               (heaping)

Meat Equivalency Comparisons	
	Usable Protein
A. If eaten separately:	*Equivalent to:*
8 cups whole wheat flour	13¾ oz steak
2 cups soy flour (or 1⅛ cups soy grits)	12 oz steak
	⎰ 25¾ oz steak
B. If eaten together: 32% increase	
8 cups wheat flour + 2 cups soy flour	
(or 1⅛ cups soy grits)	⎱ 34 oz steak

If you don't like the taste of this much soy flour in your recipes, substitute soy grits (that have been soaked briefly) for half the soy flour. Also, the soybean flour can be reduced to about ½ cup for 7 cups of wheat flour and the complementary relationship will still be effective. But remember, you won't be getting as *much* protein.

"Complementary" Pizza

four 10-inch pizzas

half of one pizza = approx. 16 g usable protein
37 to 44% of daily protein allowance

Sauce:

3 tbsp olive oil
1 cup onions, finely
   chopped
1 tbsp minced garlic
4 cups canned tomatoes,
   chopped.
1 small can tomato paste

1 tbsp dried oregano
1 tbsp fresh basil or
   1 tsp dried basil
1 bay leaf
2 tsp honey
1 tbsp salt
pepper to taste

In a 3- or 4-quart saucepan heat the oil and sauté the onions until soft but not brown. Add garlic and cook 2 minutes more. Add the remaining ingredients, bring the sauce to a boil, then lower the heat and simmer uncovered for about 1 hour, stirring occasionally. Remove bay leaf and, if a smoother sauce is desired, you may puree or sieve it.

Dough:

2 tbsp dry baking yeast
1¼ cups warm water
1 tsp honey
¼ cup olive oil

1 tsp salt
2½ cups whole wheat flour
1 cup soy flour
garnishes

Dissolve the yeast in the water with the honey. Mix with oil, salt, and flours in a large bowl. Blend well and knead until smooth and elastic on a floured board. Let rise in the bowl in a warm place until doubled in volume (about 1½ hours). Punch down and knead again for a few minutes to make dough easy to handle.

To make four 10-inch pizzas, divide the dough into quarters, stretch each quarter to a 5-inch circle while you hold it in your hands, then roll it out to 10 inches and about ⅛ inch thick. Dust pans with cornmeal, place the pizzas on top, and pinch a small rim around the edge. For each pizza use ½ cup tomato sauce, ½ cup mozzarella cheese, and 2 tbsp Parmesan. In all, you need: 1 lb mozzarella cheese, grated; and ½ cup freshly grated Parmesan cheese.

Other garnishes may top your pizza: sliced garlic, sliced onion, mushrooms, sliced green pepper.

Bake 10 to 15 minutes at 500°F.

The pizza looks like work, but it makes a wonderful supper dish—high protein in content *and* quality.

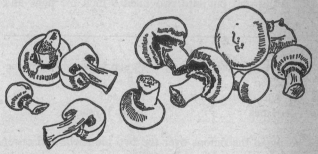

Mushrooms

Savory Onion Quiche

two 9-inch pies (12 servings)

average serving = approx. 12 g usable protein
28 to 34% of daily protein allowance

Pastry shell:

1½ cups whole wheat flour   ¼ cup oil
½ cup soy flour   1 tbsp poppy seeds
½ tsp salt   ice water

   Mix dry ingredients and oil with a pastry blender or
fork. Add just enough ice water to make a firm dough.
Roll out and put into two oiled 9-inch pie pans and
chill.

Filling:

3 cups onion, chopped and   ½ cup instant milk powder
   sautéed   4–5 eggs
2½ cups cheese, grated   1 tsp salt
3 cups milk   ½ tsp thyme

   Spread the onions over the two pie shells and cover
with the cheese. Blend the milk, milk powder, eggs, salt,
and thyme and pour over the cheese. Bake at 350°F for
25 to 30 minutes until firm.

   A superb supper dish, this quiche is especially good
with strong cheese like Port-Salut and St. Paulin mixed
with some hot pepper cheese. (When I don't have hot
pepper cheese, I like to substitute a tablespoon of finely
minced green chiles.) If using only mild cheeses, add a
dash of Worcestershire Sauce and ½ tsp dry mustard.

Wheat-Soy Waffles

about 10 waffles, 5 servings

average serving = approx. 8 g usable protein
19 to 22% of daily protein allowance

1 cup whole wheat flour	2 eggs, separated
1 tsp salt	1½ cups milk
¼ cup soy flour	3 tbsp melted butter or oil
2 tsp baking powder	2 tbsp honey

Stir dry ingredients together. Beat egg yolks, add milk, butter, and honey and blend well, stir into dry ingredients. Beat the egg whites until stiff and fold them into the batter. Bake on hot oiled waffle iron.

These are delicious, light waffles. They are especially good with the addition of about ½ cup chopped nuts, folded in with the egg whites.

Chameleon Spice Cake

12 servings

average serving with frosting: approx. 7 g usable
protein
16 to 20% of daily protein allowance

½ cups soft butter
¾ cup honey
⅔ cup brown sugar
2 eggs
Options:
1) ½ cup carob powder
   plus 1 tsp instant coffee
   mixed with ⅓ cup water,
   or
2) 1½ cups mashed
   bananas, or
3) 4 sliced apples

2 cups whole wheat flour
½ cup soy flour
1 tsp cinnamon, ground
½ tsp nutmeg, ground
½ tsp allspice, ground
1 tsp baking soda
1 tsp salt
⅔ cup buttermilk or yogurt
⅔ cup sunflower seeds or
   chopped nuts*
2 tsp vanilla extract

Cream the butter, honey, and sugar together. Add
eggs and beat until the mixture is fluffy using electric
mixer. Stir all dry ingredients together and add alternately with the vanilla and buttermilk or yogurt—beating continually with the electric mixer. Blend in option
1 or fold in by hand option 2 or 3. Stir in the nuts. Bake
at 350°F in two greased 8-inch pans or one long greased
pan. Cooking time will vary from 25 to 40 minutes.
Cake is done when toothpick comes out "clean." (To
avoid sogginess banana spice bars should be cut into
bars while still warm and cooled on a wire rack.)

* Using sunflower seeds and chopped peanuts, you can create
another complementary protein combination.

Frosting:

Cream together:
2 tbsp soft butter
1/4 cup honey
1 tsp vanilla

For carob frosting beat in:
2–3 tbsp milk or buttermilk
1/4 cup carob powder
2/3 cup instant powdered
   milk

For spice frosting beat in:
2–3 tbsp milk or buttermilk
1 cup instant powdered
   milk
dashes of cinnamon,
   nutmeg, and allspice to
   taste

Whip until smooth, adding more liquid or more powder to create desired consistency. For a fruit frosting, try substituting fruit juice for milk and adding grated orange rind instead of spices. If your child sneaks a fingerful of this frosting off the cake, you don't have to worry. It's good for him.

Honey

Wheat-Soy Pudding

about 4 servings

average serving = approx. 8 g usable protein
19 to 22% of daily protein allowance

2 cups milk
dash salt
½ cup whole wheat flour
2 tbsp honey
¼ cup raisins

2 tbsp soy flour
1 egg, separated
1 tbsp sesame seeds
2 tbsp honey

In a saucepan heat the milk, add salt, and stir in whole wheat flour. Cook over low heat, stirring constantly until the mixture is thickened. Remove from heat and stir in 2 tbsp honey, raisins, and soy flour. Beat the egg yolk and add some of the hot mixture to it, then return it to the saucepan. Beat the egg white until stiff and fold it into the hot mixture, or you can wait until it has cooled and then fold it in. Drizzle 2 more tbsp of honey over the top of the pudding, sprinkle with sesame seeds, and bake in an 8 x 8-inch pan for 25 to 30 minutes at 475°F.

Served hot or cold, this pudding is delicious with yogurt, buttermilk, cream, or milk. It is a delicious breakfast pudding too.

10. Wheat, Soy, and Sesame

Complementary Proportions

3 cups whole wheat flour **or** 2½ cups bulgur wheat	½ cup soy flour **or** ⅓ cup soybeans or grits	⅔ cup sesame seed meal **or** ½ cup sesame seeds **or** ¼ cup sesame butter

---

Meat Equivalency Comparisons

	Usable Protein Equivalent to:
A. If eaten separately:	
6½ cups whole wheat flour	11 oz steak
1 cup soybean flour	6 oz steak
1 cup sesame seed	2¾ oz steak
	19¾ oz steak
B. If eaten together: 42% increase 6½ cups whole wheat flour + 1 cup soy flour + 1 cup sesame seed	28 oz steak

Sesame Crisp Crackers

3–4 dozen crackers

1/8 of recipe = approx. 4 g usable protein
9 to 11% of daily protein allowance

1 1/2 cups whole wheat flour	3/4 tsp salt
1/4 cup soy flour	1/4 cup oil
1/4 cup sesame seeds	1/2 cup water (as needed)

Stir flours, seeds, and salt together; pour in oil and blend well. Add enough water to the dough to make it of pie dough consistency. Gather the dough into a ball, then roll it to 1/8 inch thick. Cut it in cracker shapes or sticks and place on an unoiled baking sheet. Bake at 350°F until the crackers are crisp and golden.

These crackers go well with soups as well as sweets. Be sure to serve them with your favorite dips, spreads, and cheeses.

Sesame Dream Bars

2 dozen

one bar = approx. 2 g usable protein
5 to 6% of daily protein allowance

Cookie base:
½ cup butter, softened
½ cup honey
1¼ cups whole wheat flour
¼ cup soy flour
Top layer:
2 eggs
¾ cup honey or brown
  sugar

1 tsp vanilla
¼ cup whole wheat flour
¼ tsp salt
½ tsp baking powder
½ cup shredded coconut,
  unsweetened
¼–½ cup sesame seeds

Cream the butter, add the ½ cup honey, and continue creaming the mixture until it is very light and fluffy. Add the 1¼ cups of whole wheat flour and ¼ cup soy flour, and blend well. Spread the mixture in an oiled 13x9x2-inch pan (a smaller pan will give you a cakey bar) and bake at 350°F for 15 to 20 minutes, or until firm and just beginning to brown. Cool 5 minutes before adding top layer.

For the top layer, beat eggs until light, then beat in honey (or brown sugar) and vanilla. Blend in the ¼ cup whole wheat flour, salt, and baking powder. Stir in the coconut and sesame seeds. Spread in an even layer over hot cookie base. Return to oven and bake 20 minutes more. Allow the cake to cool for about 30 minutes before cutting into squares.

Journey Cakes

8–10 cakes

average serving = approx. 7 g usable protein
16 to 20% of daily protein allowance

oil as needed
2 small onions, diced
2 cloves garlic, minced
2 small carrots, diced
2 small zucchini squash, diced
3 tbsp soy sauce
2⅔ cups whole wheat flour
⅓ cup soy flour

½ cup sesame seed meal
4 tbsp nonfat dry milk (5½ tbsp instant)
1 tbsp salt
½ cup raisins
2 tsp honey
1 egg, beaten
water

Sauté onions, garlic, and carrots in oil until the onion is golden and the carrots are tender. Add zucchini, and sauté a few minutes more, until the squash softens. Sprinkle the vegetables with soy sauce. Stir all of the dry ingredients together. Blend the vegetables, egg and honey. Combine both mixtures with enough water to make a thick batter. Spoon onto hot oiled frypan to make 6-inch-diameter cakes. Brown both sides over high heat, then lower flame to cook the cakes through.

Orange Sesame Muffins

About 9 muffins

one muffin = approx. 5 g usable protein
12 to 14% of daily protein allowance

1½ cups whole wheat flour	1 egg, beaten
½ cup soy flour	½ cup yogurt or buttermilk
1 tsp salt	¼ cup oil
2 tsp baking powder	½ cup honey
¼ cup whole sesame seeds	1 tbsp grated orange peel

Mix together flours, salt, sesame seeds, and baking powder. In a separate bowl, blend egg, yogurt, oil, and honey together. Stir in orange peel. Pour this mixture into the dry ingredients and stir just enough to moisten them. Lumps are OK. Fill muffin wells two-thirds full, and bake at 375°F about 20 minutes or until they are golden.

This fairly sweet muffin goes well with a light meal.

Wheat-Soy-Sesame Bread

2 loaves (12 slices per loaf)
one slice = approx. 4 g usable protein
9 to 11% of daily protein allowance

2 cups warm stock
1 tbsp dry baking yeast
1/4 cup oil
1/4 cup honey
1 tsp salt

3/4 cup sesame seeds
1/2 cup soy flour
2 tbsp soy grits
4–5 cups whole wheat flour

Dissolve yeast in stock, add oil, honey, salt, sesame seeds, soy flour, and grits. Add enough whole wheat flour to make a stiff dough. Knead until smooth and elastic, then set in a warm place to rise until doubled in volume (about 1½ hours). Punch down and knead a few minutes adding whole wheat flour as needed. Divide the dough in half, shape into two loaves, and place in oiled pans. Let rise for about 1 more hour or until nearly doubled, and bake at 350°F about 30 minutes.

11. Cornmeal and Beans

Complementary Proportions

1 cup cornmeal   1/4 cup beans
    or
6–7 cornmeal tortillas

Meat Equivalency Comparisons	
	Usable Protein
A. If eaten separately:	**Equivalent to:**
1/2 cup beans	2 oz steak
2 cups cornmeal	1 1/2 oz steak
	3 1/2 oz steak
B. If eaten together: 50% increase	
1/2 cup beans + 2 cups cornmeal	5 1/4 oz steak

In the recipes for this combination you'll discover *two* kinds of complementarity in the same dish! That is, the amount of beans has been increased above that which can be complemented by the cornmeal; and, to match this extra bean protein, milk protein is present, usually in the form of grated cheese. (The complementary proportions of milk and bean protein can be found in combination 13.)

Tostadas

6 servings

two tostadas = approx. 11 g usable protein
26 to 31% of daily protein allowance

Sauce:
6 medium tomatoes,
  seeded and chopped
1 cup finely chopped
  onions
2 tsp oregano, dried

½ tsp minced garlic
1 tsp honey
1 tsp salt
½ cup red wine vinegar

Combine these ingredients in a small bowl. Mix thoroughly and set aside.

Frijoles Refritos:
1½ cups dry kidney beans
5 cups water or stock
1 cup onions, chopped
2 medium tomatoes,
  chopped, or ⅔ cup
  canned

½ tsp garlic, minced
1 tsp chili powder
pinch cayenne
1 tsp salt

Soak the beans overnight, then cook them with ½ cup of the onions, ¼ cup of tomatoes, ¼ tsp of the garlic, the chili, cayenne, and 5 cups of water. When they are tender add the 1 tsp salt.

In a large frying pan, heat some oil and sauté the remaining onions and garlic until the onions are transparent. Add the tomatoes and cook 3 minutes. Mash ¼ cup of beans into the mixture with a fork. Continue mashing and adding the beans by quarter cups. Cook about 10 minutes more, then cover the pan to keep the frijoles warm.

Dressing:
1/4 cup olive oil
2 tbsp red wine vinegar
1/4 tsp salt

3 cups shredded iceberg
   lettuce

Combine the dressing ingredients and mix them together well. Drop the lettuce into the mixture and toss to coat it well.

Tortillas:
1 dozen corn tortillas

oil for frying

Fry each tortilla in oil and drain on paper towels. (Fry about 1/2 minute per side.)

To assemble the tostadas:
1 cup chopped onions

1/2 cup grated Parmesan
   cheese

Place one or two tortillas on a plate, and spread each one with 1/3 cup refried beans. Top with 1/4 cup of lettuce, some chopped onions, tomato sauce, and 2 tbsp grated cheese.

These sound like a lot of work, but most of the combinations can be made ahead of time and then quickly assembled for a delicious meal.

Enchilada Bake

4 servings

average serving = approx. 9 g usable protein
21 to 25% of daily protein allowance

½ cup dry beans, cooked
1 onion, chopped
1 clove garlic, minced
5–6 mushrooms, sliced
1 green pepper, chopped
1½ cups stewed tomatoes
1 tbsp chili powder
1 tsp cumin, ground

salt to taste
½ cup red wine
6–8 corn tortillas
½ cup grated jack cheese
½ cup mixture of ricotta
    cheese and yogurt*
black olives

Sauté onion, garlic, mushrooms, and pepper. Add the
beans, tomatoes, spices, salt, and wine. Simmer gently
for about 30 minutes. In an oiled casserole put a layer
of tortillas, a layer of sauce, 3 tbsp of grated cheese, 3
tbsp of the cheese-yogurt mixture. Repeat until all the
ingredients are used, ending with a layer of sauce. Garnish the top with the cheese-yogurt and black olives.
Bake at 350° for 15 to 20 minutes.

---

* Of course, you could use sour cream, but it has less protein. Sour cream has 82 calories per gram of usable protein
compared to 14 to 17 for ricotta and yogurt. So it's your choice!

Crusty Cornbean Pie

4–6 servings

average serving = approx. 10 g usable protein
23 to 28% of daily protein allowance

Crust:
2 cups yellow cornmeal
½ tsp salt
2 tbsp brewer's yeast
3 tbsp oil

½–¾ cup hot stock (or
   enough to make stiff
   batter)

Mix all ingredients and pat into an oiled, deep 9-inch pie or cake dish.

Filling:
oil as needed
1 onion, chopped
½ cup carrot, chopped
½ cup celery, chopped
1 cup dry kidney beans,
   cooked

pinch cayenne
1 tsp cumin, ground
¼ cup stock
3 tbsp soy sauce
⅓ cup or more of grated
   sharp cheese

Briefly sauté onion, carrot, and celery in oil. Add beans and spices and turn into the cornmeal crust. Pour stock mixed with soy sauce over the beans. Bake at 350° F about 25 minutes. Remove from oven, sprinkle with cheese, and bake 5 minutes more.

Vegetarian Enchiladas

4–6 servings

average serving = approx. 7 g usable protein
16 to 20% of daily protein allowance

Sauce:

1 cup onions, chopped
olive oil as needed
2 cups canned tomatoes
1 8-oz can tomato sauce
1 clove garlic, minced
pinch cayenne

10 drops hot sauce
1/2 tbsp chili powder
1 tbsp honey
1/2 tsp salt
1/4 tsp cumin seed, ground

Sauté onions in about 2 tbsp olive oil until golden. Add remaining ingredients and simmer, uncovered, for 30 minutes.

This is a very hot sauce. If you prefer something milder, omit the cayenne and cumin and reduce the amount of hot sauce and chili powder.

Filling:

1/2 cup dry beans, cooked
and ground
1 clove garlic, minced
1/2 cup chopped onion

2 tbsp chopped ripe olives
1 tsp chili powder
1/4 tsp salt

Sauté onion, garlic, and olives in olive oil. Add mashed or ground beans and seasonings and some of the above sauce if it seems too sticky.

To assemble: Fill six to eight *corn tortillas* with 2 to 3 tbsp of filling and 1 tbsp *grated cheese*. Place, rolled up, in a shallow baking pan. Cover with sauce, sprinkle with cheese, and garnish with black olive halves. Bake at 350°F 30 minutes till bubbling hot.

Easy Mexican Pan-Bread

4 servings

average serving = approx. 8 g usable protein
19 to 22% of daily protein allowance

½ cup dry beans, cooked
with extra water (a dark
bean such as kidney or
black bean makes the
dish colorful)
¾ cup stock from beans
1 onion, chopped
1 clove garlic, minced
1 egg, beaten

2 tsp baking powder
(optional)
1 cup cornmeal
1 tbsp chili powder, or
more to taste
½ tsp cumin, ground
½ tsp salt
⅓ cup grated cheese
¼ cup sliced black olives

Sauté onion and garlic in a small heavy skillet. Mix together all remaining ingredients *except* for the cheese and olives. Pour this mixture into the skillet and stir to mix well. Sprinkle grated cheese and olives on top and bake at 350°F for about 15 minutes. A quick delicious meal—good with soup and salad.

Variation: Serve with tomato sauce on top.

12. Cornmeal and Soy and Milk

Complementary Proportions

1 cup cornmeal	1/3 cup defatted soy flour	4 tbsp nonfat dry milk (5½ instant)
	or	or
	1/4 cup soy grits	1¼ cups milk

Meat Equivalency Comparisons

	Usable Protein Equivalent to:
A. If eaten separately:	
1 cup defatted soy flour (or 3/4 cup soy grits)	9¼ oz steak
3/4 cup nonfat dry milk	5¾ oz steak
3 cups cornmeal	2 oz steak
	————
	17 oz steak
B. If eaten together: 13% increase 1 cup defatted soy flour + 3/4 cup nonfat dry milk + 3 cups cornmeal	19¼ oz steak

My Favorite Cornbread

6 generous slices

one slice = approx. 6 g usable protein
14 to 17% of daily protein allowance

Mix together:
1 cup whole ground corn-
  meal
1/3 cup soy flour
1/4 cup whole wheat flour
2 tsp baking powder
1 tsp salt

Mix together:
1 egg
1 cup milk + 2 1/2 tbsp nonfat dry milk (3 1/2 instant)
3 tbsp honey

Add liquid mixture to dry mixture and beat until
smooth (preferably with an electric mixer). Pour into
a well oiled cake pan and bake about 30 minutes at
375°F.

Boston Brown Bread

one 2-quart loaf, 15 slices

one slice = approx. 3 g usable protein
7 to 8% daily protein allowance

1 ¾ cup whole wheat flour
1 cup cornmeal, finely
  ground, yellow
⅓ cup soy flour
1 tsp baking soda

1 tsp baking powder
1 tsp salt
¾ cup molasses
2 cups milk
1 cup raisins

Stir together the flours, baking soda, baking powder, and salt. Blend together the molasses and milk in a large bowl. Stir in the raisins and the flour mixture. Grease the insides and lids of molds or cans having tightly fitting lids (one 2-quart mold or two smaller ones). Tinfoil may be used instead of lids. Fill three-fourths full, cover, and place on a trivet in a heavy kettle over 1 inch of boiling water. Cover the kettle closely. Turn heat high until steam begins to escape and then lower heat for rest of cooking. Steam 3 hours, replenishing with hot water as needed.

Try this bread with ricotta or cream cheese mixed with chopped dates and nuts. It is dark and rich but is not at all heavy.

Pineapple-Corn Muffins

about 15 muffins

one muffin = approx. 4 g usable protein
9 to 11% of daily protein allowance

1 cup whole wheat flour
1/3 cup soy flour
3 tsp baking powder
1 tsp salt
1 cup yellow cornmeal
8 1/2 tbsp instant nonfat dry
   milk (about 1/2 cup)*
2 eggs, beaten
1 cup water (or part water

and part liquid from
   pineapple)
1/4 cup butter, melted
2 tbsp honey
8 oz crushed pineapple
   (unsweetened), drained
pineapple preserves (or
   orange marmalade)

Stir together all the dry ingredients, including the dry milk. Combine all the remaining ingredients (except preserves) and stir into dry ingredients. Don't overmix. Fill oiled muffin wells about 2/3 full and top with 1/4 to 1/2 tsp pineapple preserves. Bake at 400°F for about 20 minutes, or until golden. Since these muffins are not very sweet they can be served with the main course. For a dessert muffin you might wish to add more honey.

---

* There is enough milk powder here to meet the complementary proportions of the corn-soy combination and still have some left to complement the wheat flour.

Corn Spice Coffee Cake

6–8 servings

average serving = approx. 4 g usable protein
9 to 11% of daily protein allowance

1 cup fine cornmeal	1½ tsp baking powder
⅓ cup soy flour	½ tsp cinnamon
4 tbsp nonfat dry milk (5½ instant)	½ tsp nutmeg
	pinch salt
½ cup whole wheat flour	1 cup raisins
1 cup brown sugar	¼ cup vegetable oil

(buttermilk and applesauce for topping)

Mix oil, raisins, salt, and spices in 1¼ cups water and simmer. When cool add to dry ingredients. Mix well. Pour into a well greased loaf pan or cake pan and bake 1 hour at 375°F.

Top with a thick sauce made by combining applesauce and buttermilk. Delicious as a breakfast dish or dessert.

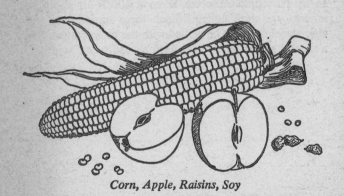

Corn, Apple, Raisins, Soy

Cornmeal-Soy Waffles

6 waffles

two waffles = approx. 13 g usable protein
30 to 36% of daily protein allowance

2 eggs
1 cup milk + 1 tbsp nonfat
   dry milk
3 tbsp oil
3 tbsp molasses
1 cup cornmeal

1/3 cup soy flour
1/2 tsp salt
2 tsp baking powder
oil as needed for the waffle
   iron

Beat eggs, add milk, oil, and molasses and blend well. Stir together cornmeal, soy flour, salt, and baking powder. Add to first mixture and blend well. Bake in hot, oiled waffle iron using about 1/2 cup of batter per waffle.

These are surprisingly delicious waffles, golden and crunchy, easy to make.

Indian Pudding

4–6 servings

average serving = approx. 12 g usable protein
28 to 34% of daily protein allowance

4 cups milk
1 cup yellow cornmeal
1/4 cup soy grits soaked in
  1/2 cup water
1/3 cup butter (fill a cup 2/3
  full of water, then add
  butter till cup is brim-
  ming; drain off water)
1/2 cup brown sugar

2/3 cup light molasses
3/4 tsp salt
1/2 tsp cinnamon, ground
1/4 tsp cloves, ground
1/4 tsp ginger, ground
1/8 tsp allspice, ground
1/8 tsp nutmeg, ground
2 eggs, beaten

Bring milk to a boil, add cornmeal and soy grits gradually. Lower heat and beat with a wire whisk to maintain a smooth mixture. When mixture begins to thicken remove from heat. Add remaining ingredients *except* eggs and allow to cool slightly. Blend in the beaten eggs, pour into a buttered baking dish, and bake 45 to 60 minutes in a 325°F oven, or until pudding is firm.

This pudding is delicious both hot and cold, especially with yogurt, sour cream, or ice cream. For variation you may add 1/2 cup of dried fruit and omit the sugar.

13. Beans and Milk

Complementary Proportions

cup beans | 1/2 cup (scant) nonfat dry milk (2/3 instant)
or
2 cups skim milk
or
2 1/2 oz cheese (2/3 cup grated)

Meat Equivalency Comparisons	
	Usable Protein
A. If eaten separately:	*Equivalent to:*
1/2 cup (scant) nonfat dry milk	3 1/3 oz steak
1 cup beans	4 1/4 oz steak
	7 1/2 oz steak
B. If eaten together: 11% increase	
1/2 cup (scant) nonfat dry milk +	
1 cup beans	8 1/3 oz steak

Although garbanzo beans (also known as chick peas) and black beans are most often used in experimental tests, these figures undoubtedly hold true for other beans and peas as well—since the amino acid patterns of legumes as a group are so similar.

Minestrone con Crema

6–8 servings

average serving = approx. 10 g usable protein
23 to 28% of daily protein allowance

¾ cup dry garbanzos,
cooked until almost done

PESTO:
½ cup fresh basil, spinach,
or parsley leaves (dry
leaves won't work)
1 clove garlic, minced
1 cup grated Parmesan
cheese
olive oil as needed

5 kohlrabi or turnips with
leaves chopped (about 2
cups) and bulbs diced
1 head cabbage, finely
chopped or grated
2 cups beet greens or
spinach, without stems,
chopped
¼ cup parsley
salt to taste
3 cups milk
sherry to taste (optional)

Make a pesto: Mash together in a mortar, or put in a blender, the fresh basil, garlic, and Parmesan cheese with enough olive oil to make a smooth paste.

Put all the vegetables in a pot with the beans and cooking water from beans—plus just enough water to cover. (Seem like a lot of vegetables? Believe me, it works!) Add the parsley and salt, bring to a boil, then simmer about 1 hour. Add the milk and simmer the soup 15 minutes more. Stir in the pesto (and sherry, optional) and heat 5 minutes more. Serve at once. This soup is truly delicious. (A friend who swears that he dislikes both greens and turnips ate this soup with gusto!)

Savory Stuffed Peppers

6 servings

average serving = approx. 7 g usable protein
16 to 20% of daily protein allowance

1 cup dry beans, cooked
    and mashed
oil as needed
1/2 onion, chopped
1/2 cup celery, chopped
2 cups tomatoes, canned,
    or 3 fresh tomatoes,
    chopped
1/2 tsp basil

1 tbsp parsley, chopped
salt to taste
liquid from canned
    tomatoes or water—as
    needed
6 green peppers, seeds and
    membranes removed
2/3 cup cheese, grated,
    more as needed

Sauté the onion and celery in the oil until the onion
is transparent. Stir in the tomatoes, mashed beans, and
herbs, and add liquid if the mixture is very dry. Remove
from heat and stir in the 2/3 cup grated cheese, and salt
to taste. Fill the prepared peppers with the mixture and
bake at 400° F in a pan with 1 inch of hot water in the
bottom. Check to be sure the pan doesn't dry out during the 25 to 30 minutes of baking. During the last 10
minutes of baking, sprinkle more grated cheese on top
of peppers.

Bean-Vegetable Casserole

3 servings

average serving = approx. 7 g usable protein
16 to 20% of daily protein allowance

½ cup dry garbanzo or
  other beans
2 cups stock
1 bay leaf
1 tsp basil
1 tsp sage
10 peppercorns
1 tsp salt

1 clove garlic, crushed
¼ lb string beans, sliced
  into 2-inch pieces
2 large tomatoes, sliced
⅓ cup grated cheese, or
  more
butter

Soak the beans overnight in the stock with bay leaf, basil, sage, pepper, and garlic. Cook the beans with seasonings until tender, remove the peppercorns, and add salt. (You may also remove the bay leaf and garlic.) In an oiled casserole alternate layers of the drained beans, string beans, tomatoes, and cheese, ending with cheese. Dot with butter and bake in a 350°F oven for 30 minutes.

Garbanzo Cheese Salad

4–5 servings

average serving = approx. 8 g usable protein
19 to 22% of daily protein allowance

½ cup dry garbanzo beans,
cooked and cooled
½ bunch red leaf lettuce,
torn up
½ bunch spinach, torn
½ cup scallions, sliced
1 green pepper, chopped
½ cup fresh raw shelled
peas

½ cup raw yellow crooked-
neck squash, diced or
sliced
½ cup cucumber, chopped
or sliced
1 cup bean or alfalfa
sprouts
⅔ cup cheese, grated

Combine all ingredients, sprinkle with favorite dressing, and serve on a bed of greens.

Naturally, you can use any combination of fresh vegetables that are available, just be sure to include the garbanzo beans and cheese.

Creamy Garbanzos

4 servings

average serving = approx. 10 g usable protein
23 to 28% of daily protein allowance

1 cup dry garbanzos,
  cooked (save 2 cups
  stock)

oil as needed
2 cups onions, minced

Sauté onions in oil until they are transparent. Chop or coarsely grind garbanzos if desired and stir together with the onions. Place this mixture in a small oiled casserole.

---

4 tbsp oil
4 tbsp whole wheat flour
2 tsp salt
2 cups stock from beans

½ cup (scant)
  dry milk (add 4 tbsp
  more if instant)

Heat the oil in a small saucepan, add the flour and, stirring constantly, brown it until it is toasted and nutty smelling. Blend the milk and stock and add to the browned flour. Simmer, stirring often, until thickened. Stir in salt. Pour the sauce over the beans in the casserole and bake for 30 minutes in a 350°F oven. Sprinkle chopped parsley on top.

14. Beans and Sesame Seeds

Complementary Proportions

1/3 cup garbanzo beans   1/2 cup sesame seed
                           or
                           3/4 cup sesame meal
                           or
                           1/4 cup sesame butter

Meat Equivalency Comparisons	
	Usable Protein Equivalent to:
A. If eaten separately:	
1 cup garbanzo beans	4 1/4 oz steak
1 1/2 cups sesame seeds	4 oz steak
	8 1/4 oz steak
B. If eaten together: 27% increase	
1 cup garbanzo beans +	
1 1/2 cups sesame seeds	10 1/2 oz steak

This combination is presented in terms of garbanzo beans and sesame seeds because they are most frequently used in experiments to determine complementarity. However, the substitution of other beans or peas for garbanzos and sunflower seeds for sesame seeds would probably result in similar complementary effects.

Garbanzo Snacks

about 1½ cups

⅛ cup = approx. 4 g usable protein
9 to 11% of daily protein allowance

1 cup dry garbanzo beans,
  cooked
2 tbsp butter
2 cloves garlic, crushed
1½ cups sesame seeds,
  lightly roasted

¼–½ tsp garlic or onion
  salt (optional)
¼ tsp dry mustard, ½ tsp
  chili powder, and 1 tsp
  salt, or ½ tsp ground
  ginger and 1½ tsp soy
  sauce

Melt the butter in a heavy skillet, sauté the garlic, and then add the cooked garbanzos. Sauté slowly, stirring often, until garbanzos are golden brown and sizzling. They should be crunchy, but tender on the inside. Mix them with the sesame seeds (and garlic or onion salt). Blend in *either* the mustard, chili, and salt *or* ginger and soy sauce. Eat hot if possible.

These snacks can be easily frozen. To reheat, do not defrost, but spread on a cookie sheet and run under the broiler until sizzling and crisp.

Garbanzo Paté

4 servings

average serving = approx. 11 g usable protein
26 to 31% of daily protein allowance

2 cups bread or bread
   crumbs (stale is all right)
2 cups hot stock or water
oil as needed
2 chopped onions
1/2 cup sesame seed meal
2 tbsp sesame butter
1/8 tsp each thyme, cori-
   ander, and nutmeg

1 bay leaf
1/2 tsp salt
1/4 cup chopped parsley
3 tbsp soy sauce
2/3 cup dry garbanzos,
   cooked and pureed
2/3 cup grated cheese

Soak bread in hot stock while you prepare vegetables. Sauté onions in the oil until golden. Add sesame meal and butter. Cook until lightly browned. Stir in bread and stock mixture. Cook until the mixture thickens, about 15 minutes. Add spices and herbs. Cook 5 minutes. Add pureed garbanzos. Stir. Put in loaf pan and cook 30 minutes at 325°F. Add cheese on top in last ten minutes. Good hot or cold (or as a good sandwich spread).

Garbanzos in excess of the proportions in this combination are complemented by the milk protein in the cheese.

Middle Eastern Tacos

10 tacos

2 tacos = approx. 10 g usable protein
23 to 28% of daily protein allowance

1 cup dry garbanzo beans, cooked

½ cup (heaping) sesame seeds, toasted

2 cloves garlic

2 tbsp lemon juice

¾ tsp coriander, ground

½ tsp salt

½ tsp cumin, ground

¼–½ tsp cayenne

10 pieces Middle Eastern flat bread or 10 wheat tortillas

Puree together all ingredients (increase spices to taste). Let stand at least ½ hour at room temperature. Cut pieces of Middle Eastern flat bread in half and fill "pockets" with bean mixture; or serve on wheat tortillas, fried until soft but not crisp. Add the following garnishes and allow everyone at the table to assemble their own "taco";

shredded lettuce

chopped tomatoes

chopped cucumber

chopped onion

1½ cups yogurt (or cheese)

Wonderfully tasty and satisfying! Be sure to include yogurt or cheese on each portion to complete the protein complementarity.

Garbanzo Patties

4 servings

average serving = approx. 7 g usable protein
16 to 20% of daily protein allowance

1/3 cup dry garbanzo beans, cooked
oil as needed
3/4 cup sesame meal
1/4 cup brewer's yeast

2 green peppers, finely chopped
2 onions chopped
1/4 lb mushrooms, finely chopped
juice of one lemon

Mash the cooked garbanzos and mix with lemon juice. Blend with remaining ingredients and shape into patties. Dip into raw wheat germ flakes and fry in hot oil quickly until just heated through. Do not overcook. (Hot or cold these patties make a good sandwich with lettuce, tomato, and your favorite dressing.)

15. Soy, Wheat, Rice, and Peanuts

Complementary Proportions

1/3 cup soy-beans or grits **or** 1/2 cup soy flour	1/4 cup pea-nuts **or** 1/8 cup pea-nut butter	2/3 cup bulgur wheat **or** 3/4 cup whole wheat flour	3/4 cup rice

---

Meat Equivalency Comparisons

	Usable Protein Equivalent to:
A. If eaten separately:	
1/3 cup soybeans	3 1/4 oz steak
1/4 cup peanuts	1 oz steak
2/3 cup bulgur	1 oz steak
3/4 cup rice	1 1/3 oz steak
	——————
	6 1/2 oz steak
B. If eaten together: 15% increase	
1/3 cup soybeans + 1/4 cup peanuts + 2/3 cups bulgur + 3/4 cup rice	7 1/2 oz steak

Curried Soybeans and Peanuts

4 servings

**average serving = approx. 11 g usable protein
26 to 31% of daily protein allowance**

1/3 cup dry soybeans, cooked with: 1/4 cup raw peanuts	1/2 tsp ground fresh ginger
	1–1 1/2 cups yogurt
1 tbsp curry powder	paprika
1 apple, finely chopped	soy sauce
1 onion, finely chopped	bay leaf
	oil

Sauté the curry powder, apple, and onion in a little oil until the onion is transparent. Stir in beans and peanuts which have been cooked with a bay leaf. Stir in ginger, and paprika and soy sauce to taste. Remove to a serving dish and stir in the yogurt. (If you stir the yogurt into the hot saucepan, it will curdle.)

Serve the curried beans over: 2/3 cup dry bulgur wheat, cooked with 3/4 cup dry brown rice and 1 tsp tarragon.

Once the beans and peanuts are cooked this dish is really easy to put together, and delicious as well.

Nutty Bean Tacos

makes 5–6

one serving (2 tacos) = approx. 13 g usable protein
30 to 36% of daily protein allowance

½ cup dry soybeans
  (cooked tender)
⅛ cup chopped peanuts
⅓ cup raw rice (cooked)
⅓ cup raw bulgur (cooked)
2 cloves minced garlic

½ green pepper, diced
1 tsp salt
¼–½ tsp chili powder
¼ cup tomato sauce
about 6 corn tortillas

Garnishes: shredded lettuce, chopped scallions, chopped
  tomato, grated cheese

(Peanuts, rice, and bulgur may be cooked together.) Puree cooked soybeans in blender. Mix first four ingredients together with the remaining ingredients, adding just enough tomato sauce to achieve desired consistency. Fry corn tortillas according to directions on package. Fill with mixture. Garnish as you please and top with taco sauce. Very satisfying!

This recipe makes two complete complementary protein combinations. Part of the soybeans, the peanuts, the bulgur, and the rice make one combination. The rest of the soybeans and the corn in the tortillas make another!

Soybean Croquettes

4 servings

average serving = approx. 14 g usable protein
32 to 39% daily protein allowance

1/3 cup dry soybeans
(soaked overnight)
1 onion, chopped
1 bay leaf
1 tsp salt
2 tomatoes, peeled,
seeded, and chopped
1/4 cup peanuts
3/4 cup walnuts

1 onion, cut in large chunks
for blender or minced by
hand
2 tsp butter
2 eggs, well beaten
bread crumbs or raw wheat
germ
3/4 cup raw brown rice
2/3 cup raw bulgur wheat

Bean mixture: Either: Cook soaked beans * with the chopped onion, bay leaf, and salt, adding tomatoes in the last 10 minutes of cooking; *or:* pressure unsoaked beans * with bay leaf and onion. Add slightly stewed tomatoes to cooked beans. Drain liquid (save for future soups). Mash slightly.

Nut mixture: Either: Blend together in an electric blender peanuts, walnuts, cut-up onion, and butter just until nuts are ground; *or:* grind nuts in a mortar and blend by hand with minced onion and butter. Combine both mixtures. Combination should be quite moist but if *too* moist add bread crumbs. Form into balls, dip in egg, and roll in wheat germ or bread crumbs. Bake at 400°F until brown, about 30 minutes. Serve on a bed of rice and bulgur which have been prepared according to the sauté method.* Pour a cheese sauce, Italian tomato sauce, or any favorite sauce over the croquettes and grains, and you have an elegant dish.

* See Basic Cooking Instructions, Appendix A.

Spanish Soybeans over Mixed Grains

6–8 servings

average serving = approx. 13 g usable protein
30 to 36% of daily protein allowance

⅔ cup dry soybeans
  cooked with ½ cup raw
  peanuts
2 cups stewed tomatoes
3 tbsp oil
1 onion chopped (or 1 cup)
1 green pepper, chopped
1 tsp soy flour

1 tsp salt
pinch cayenne
3 tbsp brewer's yeast
1 tsp oregano
1 tsp celery seeds, ground
1⅓ cups raw bulgur and
  1½ cups raw brown rice,
  cooked together

Combine all ingredients except the mixed bulgur and rice. Simmer 15 minutes. Serve over the mixed grains.

Deep Dish Vegetable Pie

6 servings

average serving = approx. 8 g usable protein
19 to 22% of daily protein allowance

Crust*:

1 cup whole wheat flour	1 tsp salt
1 scant cup brown rice flour (grind very finely ¾ cup brown rice)	½ cup butter, softened
	2–3 tbsp water

Stir together flours and salt, cut in shortening, and add enough water so that the dough can be gathered into a ball. Roll dough to ⅛ inch and line an 8-inch cake dish. Chill at least 2 hours. Save the excess dough for a lattice top crust. Bake the empty shell for 5 minutes at 350°F.

Filling:

1 cup broccoli pieces	¼ cup raw peanuts, cooked
1 cup cabbage, shredded	¼ cup oil
1 cup carrots, chopped	¼ cup whole wheat flour
1 cup cauliflowerettes	2 cups stock
1 onion, chopped	½ tsp basil
½ cup celery, chopped	½ tsp dill seed, ground
½ cup mushrooms, chopped	½ tsp oregano
¼ cup chopped parsley	½ tsp salt
⅓ cup dry soybeans, cooked	1 egg, beaten

* If you don't want to bake a pie crust, you can prepare the vegetables as above and bake them in an oiled casserole. Serve them over ¾ cup raw brown rice cooked with ⅔ cup raw bulgur wheat.

After you have prepared all of the vegetables, stir them together with the soybeans and peanuts, mixing well. Turn the mixture into the prebaked pie shell.

Make a cream sauce of the oil, flour, and stock. While it thickens, add the herbs and salt. Stir a little of the hot sauce into the beaten egg, then return this mixture to the rest of the sauce.

Pour the sauce over the vegetables in the crust, moving the vegetables, if necessary, to distribute the sauce well.

Make a lattice or top crust with the remaining dough. Bake the pie at 350°F for 45 to 60 minutes, until the crust is lightly browned and the pie is bubbling.

For this hearty pie, you can use any fresh vegetables available. Just be sure to include the soybeans and peanuts, and to use a rice-wheat crust or the mixed grains.

16. Soy and Sesame Seeds* and Peanuts

Complementary Proportions

1 cup soy flour or 2/3 cup soybeans or grits	1¾ cups sesame seeds or 2⅓ cups sesame meal or ⅞ cup sesame butter	8 oz raw peanuts (about 1½ cups) or ⅞ cup peanut butter or 2 cups ground peanuts

---

Meat Equivalency Comparisons

	Usable Protein Equivalent to:
A. If eaten separately:	
2/3 cup soybeans	6 oz steak
1¾ cups sesame seeds	4¾ oz steak
1½ cups peanuts	6½ oz steak
	_____
	17¼ oz steak
B. If eaten together: 25% increase 2/3 cup soybeans + 1¾ cups sesame seeds + 1½ cups peanuts	
	21½ oz steak

---

* You may wish to substitute sunflower seeds for sesame
seeds. The same complementary effects would probably hold
true. See complementary combination 5 for explanation.

Nutty Noodle Casserole

8–10 servings

average serving = approx. 15 g usable protein
35 to 42% of daily protein allowance

12 oz noodles (whole wheat
or soy noodles, if possi-
ble), cooked and drained
2/3 cup dry soybeans,
cooked
1/2 cup butter
2 medium onions, chopped
1 1/2 cups peanuts

1 cup cashews
2 cups yogurt (or more)
2/3 cup raw sesame butter
1/2 cup sesame meal,
toasted
salt and pepper to taste
1 tsp nutmeg (or more)

Sauté onions in butter until transparent. Add the peanuts and cashews; stir until all the ingredients are lightly browned. Then combine with the noodles and soybeans and place in a 350°F oven until thoroughly heated. Remove to a serving dish or casserole and stir in the sesame butter, yogurt, and nutmeg which have been thoroughly blended. Season with salt and pepper and sprinkle sesame seed meal over the top.

A simple variation is to stir the sesame seeds into the mixture when adding the yogurt–sesame butter blend.

Soy-Sesame-Peanut Spread

about 2 cups

⅛ cup serving = approx. 3 g usable protein
7 to 8% of daily protein allowance

½ cup soy flour, roasted in a dry pan until lightly browned
slightly more than ⅓ cup peanut butter
1⅛ cups toasted sesame seed meal or ½ cup sesame
  butter
salt

Blend together, adding enough water or other liquid
to make a good consistency for spreading. Use like any
nut butter. Add garlic or onion powder (or chopped
onions), herbs, either fresh or dried and soaked. To
let the flavors mingle, be sure to let the herbed mixture
stand at room temperature at least 1 hour before serving. Spread on rye bread and grill lightly with sliced
tomato—especially delicious. The spread can also be
sweetened with fruit juice or honey; or it can be thinned
with your favorite salad dressing to use as a vegetable
sauce or salad dressing.

This spread can also be the basis of a delicious loaf
fit for a company dinner. See the following recipe.

Peanut-Sesame Loaf Supreme

4 servings

average serving = 12 g usable protein
28 to 34% of daily protein allowance

1 cup of soy-sesame-peanut spread (see preceding recipe)
2 cloves garlic, minced
1/2 small onion
1 egg
salt, if needed
1 cup raw bulgur, cooked according to sauté method with: 8 large mushrooms, chopped

Sauce*:
1 tbsp butter
1 tbsp flour (or more if needed)
1/2 small onion, finely chopped
1 cup milk
salt and pepper to taste

Garnish:
chopped parsley

Blend spread with garlic, onion, and egg. Stir into cooked bulgur and mushroom mixture until thoroughly mixed. Pack into oiled small loaf pan. (To be sure that the loaf will come out easily, line the bottom of the pan with tinfoil.) Bake at 350°F for 25 minutes. Or, for a quicker meal, shape the mixture into small patties, roll in wheat germ, and fry on a hot griddle.

While the loaf is baking, make a cream sauce in the top of a double boiler. Melt butter and add flour. Stir into paste. Add onion and milk, stirring with a whisk to avoid lumps. Add salt and pepper, and continue cooking to desired thickness.

Turn loaf out on a platter and pour sauce over top. Sprinkle with chopped parsley. This loaf has a rich and very pleasing taste!

---

* If you are not going to make the sauce, be sure to add 2½ tbsp of nonfat dry milk (3½ instant) to the loaf mixture to complement the bulgur.

Soy-Pea Sesame Snacks

4 cups

1/4 cup = approx. 6 g usable protein
14 to 17% of daily protein allowance

2/3 cup dry soybeans, cooked

2 tbsp butter

2 cloves garlic, crushed

1 1/2 cups peanuts, roasted

1 3/4 cups sesame seeds, lightly roasted

1/2–1 tsp garlic or onion salt (optional)

1/2 tsp dry mustard, 1 tsp chili powder, 2 tsp salt, or 1 tsp ginger, ground, 1 tbsp soy sauce

---

Melt the butter in a heavy skillet. Sauté the garlic a minute or two, then add the soybeans and stir over a low heat until they are browned and sizzling. Mix them together with the peanuts and sesame seeds (and garlic or onion salt). Combine the mixed nuts and beans with a mixture of *either* dry mustard, chili powder, and salt *or* ginger and soy sauce. Eat hot.

You can make these snacks ahead of time and freeze them. To reheat, spread out the frozen mixture on a cookie sheet and heat quickly under the broiler until sizzling.

Bean Burgers

4 servings

average serving = 18 g usable protein
42 to 50% of daily protein allowance

¾ cup raw peanuts, cooked
  and pureed
⅓ cup dry soybeans,
  cooked and pureed
½ cup toasted sesame
  seed meal
½ cup toasted sunflower
  seeds*
1 onion, grated
1 carrot, grated
1 stalk celery, chopped
2 cloves garlic, crushed or
  minced
1 egg, beaten
3 tbsp brewer's yeast
½ tsp salt
½ tsp dill seed, ground
½ cup cooked brown rice

After preparing all of the ingredients, combine them and shape into patties. Brown on both sides in a little oil. These are tasty with any tomato sauce or even ketchup!

For variation, especially if you are cooking for several people, pack the mixture into a loaf pan and bake at 350°F until a nice crust is formed.

Before being browned or baked, the mixture can be used for a delicious sandwich spread. And you will find that the cold burgers (or loaf slices) make wonderful sandwiches with cheese, lettuce, and ketchup!

---

* As I explained earlier, the substitution of sunflower seed for sesame seed will probably result in similar complementary effects.

17. Peanuts and Sunflower Seeds

Complementary Proportions

1 cup sunflower seeds	¾ cup peanuts
or	or
1¼ cups sunflower meal	½ cup (scant) peanut butter

Meat Equivalency Comparisons

	Usable Protein Equivalent to:
A. If eaten separately:	
¾ cup peanuts	3 oz steak
1 cup sunflower seeds	3¾ oz steak
	6¾ oz steak
B. If eaten together: 19% increase	
¾ cup peanuts + 1 cup sunflower seeds	8 oz steak

Fine Fruit Salad and Other Ideas

8 servings

average serving = approx. 5 g usable protein
12 to 14% of daily protein allowance

¾ cup peanuts, roasted
1 cup sunflower seeds, raw
  or roasted
1 cup apples, sliced
1 cup bananas, sliced
½ cup tangerine or orange
  sections
1 cup fresh peaches, sliced

1 cup seedless grapes
½ cup raisins
½ cup shredded coconut
2–4 tbsp honey
juice of ½ lemon
½ cup wine
10–15 leaves fresh mint

Combine all ingredients in a large bowl and mix thoroughly. Garnish with mint leaves. At different times of the year you can substitute any fruit in season. Just be sure to include the peanuts and sunflower seeds for complementarity.

Other delicious salad ideas using peanuts and sunflower seeds:

Peanut-Sunflower-Carrot Salad:

Just combine grated carrots, raisins, peanuts, sunflower seeds, and crushed pineapple (optional) with a dressing of one part peanut butter to two parts mayonnaise.

Peanut-Sunflower Waldorf Salad:

Sprinkle lemon juice over diced apples (or pineapple chunks) and celery. Add chopped peanuts and sunflower seeds. Moisten with a dressing of blended mayonnaise and peanut butter.

Nutty Applesauce Cake (or Banana Bread)

sixteen 2-inch squares

one square = approx. 3 g* usable protein
7 to 8% of daily protein allowance

1 cup applesauce
¾ cup honey
⅓ cup oil or melted butter
1¼ cups whole wheat flour
⅓ cup soy flour
1 tsp baking soda

½ tsp each salt, cinnamon,
  ginger, cloves
⅓–⅔ cup roasted peanuts,
  ground†
½–1 cup sunflower seeds†

Mix together the applesauce, honey, and oil. Stir together the remaining ingredients and blend into the liquid. Bake in an 8-inch-square pan for 30 minutes at 350°F. The pan should be oiled and floured.

Variation: Substitute two ripe mashed bananas, 1 tsp vanilla, and 1 egg for the applesauce. Reduce honey to ½ cup and delete spices (but not salt). (Peanuts may be chopped instead of ground for this recipe.) Bake at 350°F in a small oiled bread pan for about 1 hour. Banana and peanut is an especially good taste combination.

---

* Based on lesser amounts of nuts and seeds.
† The larger amount of nuts and seeds makes a very nutty cake, but will increase the amount of protein. Notice that the wheat and soy flour also complement each other.

Party Snacks

4½ cups, 18 servings

average serving = approx. 3 g usable protein
7 to 8% of daily protein allowance

¾ cup peanuts, roasted
1 cup sunflower seeds,
  roasted
1 cup cashews, roasted

1 cup raisins
1 cup coconut shreds,
  toasted
salt (optional)

Combine all ingredients and serve as a party snack. This also makes a simple dessert after a big meal. You can vary the recipe by leaving all of the ingredients raw. Try substituting sliced dates for the raisins and walnuts for the cashews. This makes a richer snack.

Sunflower and seeds

Chocolate Chip Cookies

about 60 cookies

one cookie = approx. 1.5 g usable protein
3 to 4% of daily protein allowance

2¼ cups whole wheat flour
1 tsp soda
1 tsp salt
½ cup soft butter
1½ cups brown sugar,
  packed
3 eggs, beaten
1 tsp vanilla

4½ tbsp dry milk powder
  (6 tbsp instant)
1 tbsp water
12 oz semi-sweet chocolate
  chips
¾ cup peanuts, chopped
1 cup sunflower seeds

Stir flour, soda, and salt together and set aside. In a large bowl, cream the butter with the sugar. Add eggs, vanilla, milk powder and water. Beat until fluffy. Add the flour mixture and blend well. Stir in chocolate chips, nuts, and seeds. Drop by tablespoonsful onto greased cookie sheet. Bake at 375°F for 10 to 15 minutes or until browned.

Remember you can add complementary protein ingredients to any cake or cookie recipe that calls for nuts. Just add peanuts and sunflower seeds in the proper proportions in place of the nuts or seeds called for in the recipe.

Tiger's Candy

2 dozen balls

two balls = approx. 3 g usable protein
7 to 8% of daily protein allowance

½ cup peanut butter*
⅔ cup sunflower seed meal
¼ cup raisins, chopped fine
¼ cup dates, chopped fine
1 tbsp brewer's yeast

2 tbsp dry milk
   (3½ tbsp instant)
1 tbsp honey
carob powder or shredded
   coconut

In a small bowl, blend the peanut butter and sunflower seed meal. Stir in the brewer's yeast, dry milk, and honey. Then add the raisins and dates. Probably the easiest way to blend all of the ingredients is by using your hands. If the mixture is too dry, add liquid milk; if too wet, add more powdered milk. Roll into balls and roll in coconut or carob powder. Chill.

---

* The peanut butter in excess of the proportions given is complemented by the dry milk.

18. Peanuts, Milk and Wheat

Complementary Proportions

(a) 1 cup peanut butter   5 tbsp nonfat dry milk (7 instant)
    or   or
1¾ cups peanuts   1½ cups skim milk
                    or

(b) ½ cup peanut   4 tbsp nonfat dry   3¾ cups whole
     butter   milk (5½ instant)   wheat flour
    or   or
⅞ cup peanuts   ¼ cup soy flour

Meat Equivalency Comparisons

	Usable Protein Equivalent to:
(a) Peanut–Milk	
A. If eaten separately:	
5 tbsp nonfat dry milk	2⅓ oz steak
1 cup peanut butter	7 oz steak
	9⅓ oz steak
B. If eaten together: 25% increase	
5 tbsp nonfat dry milk +	
1 cup peanut butter	11⅔ oz steak
(b) Peanut–Milk (or Soy)–Whole Wheat	
A. If eaten separately:	
1 cup peanut butter	7 oz. steak
½ cup nonfat dry milk or soy flour	3 oz steak
7½ cups whole wheat flour	12¾ oz steak
	22¾ oz steak
B. If eaten together: 34% increase	
1 cup peanut butter + ½ cup nonfat dry milk or soy flour + 7½ cups whole wheat flour	30½ oz steak

Peanut Butter Sauce

about 2 cups

¼ cup = 2 g usable protein
5 to 6% of daily protein allowance

½ cup peanut butter
1 onion, grated
1 clove garlic, crushed
2½ tbsp skim milk powder
  (or 3½ tbsp instant)

¼ tsp honey
2–4 tbsp lemon juice
4 tbsp soy sauce

Blend all ingredients and add hot water until the mixture has the consistency of heavy cream. If you wish a very smooth sauce, blend the mixture in a blender with the hot water.

Serve over hot or cold tofu (soy curd) or with cooked grains and vegetables.

Peanut Butter Log

one 10-inch log

1-inch slice = approx. 3 g usable protein
7 to 8% of daily protein allowance

½ cup peanut butter
2½ tbsp nonfat dry milk (3½ instant)—more as needed
½ cup raisins
2 tbsp honey (optional)

Blend peanut butter (and honey), then work in as much powdered milk as you need to make the mixture easy to handle and fairly stiff. Pick up the mixture and knead in the raisins, distributing them evenly. Roll into a 1-inch thick and 10-inch long log. Chill and slice or pull apart.

This mixture can be molded into any shape and even pressed into cookie molds to make an exciting snack for small children (and big ones too).

Peanut Butter Corn Sticks

12 sticks

each stick = approx. 3 g usable protein
7 to 8% of daily protein allowance

1 cup whole wheat flour	1/4 cup peanut butter
1 tbsp baking powder	2 tbsp honey
1/2 tsp salt	1 egg, beaten
1/2 cup yellow cornmeal	2/3 cup milk

Stir the dry ingredients together in a mixing bowl. Blend the peanut butter with honey, egg, and milk in a blender *or* cut the peanut butter into the dry ingredients with a knife and combine the honey, milk, and egg. Stir the liquid into the dry ingredients, fill oiled corn stick, gem, or shallow muffin pans two-thirds full. Bake at 425°F 12 to 15 minutes.

These corn sticks are not too sweet. They accompany vegetable soups or stews very nicely.

This recipe fits the complementary proportions for combination 18(*a*), but there is extra milk present to complement the cup of wheat flour.

PeaConut Snacks

about 1 dozen

two pieces = approx. 3 g usable protein
7 to 8% of daily protein allowance

1/4 cup peanut butter
2 tbsp honey (or more to taste)
2 tbsp water blended with:
2 tbsp instant milk powder
coconut, grated unsweetened, roasted or raw according to
    your taste*

In a small saucepan blend all of the ingredients *except* coconut. Stir over a low heat until the mixture is very thick. Remove from heat and stir in enough coconut to hold the mixture together so it will form into balls. Roll into twelve 1-inch balls (or whatever size you prefer) and roll in more coconut. Chill several hours.

---

* In this quick snack I usually use raw coconut stirred into the mixture and roll the balls in toasted coconut. For toasted coconut, buy shredded or grated unsweetened coconut in your health food store (you will be surprised at how much cheaper it is than the packaged and sugared products). Toast it in a dry pan on top of the stove over low heat, stirring constantly.

Peanut Butter Cookies with a Difference

about 30 cookies

one cookie = approx. 2 g usable protein
5 to 6% of daily protein allowance

½ cup oil	½ tsp salt
1 cup honey	1 tsp cinnamon
¾ cup peanut butter	½ tsp mace
2 eggs, beaten	¼ tsp cloves
5½ tbsp skim milk powder (7½ instant)	½ cup rolled oats
	½ cup raisins
2 tsp baking powder	¾ cup whole wheat flour

In a large bowl with an electric mixer blend oil and honey several minutes until they get creamy and light. Add the peanut butter and continue beating until the mixture is blended. Beat in eggs, milk powder, baking powder, salt, and spices. At this point the batter will be very thick and gluey, so do the rest of the mixing with a wooden spoon. Stir in the oats, raisins, and whole wheat flour, making sure everything is well blended. Drop by teaspoons on an unoiled cookie sheet. Bake 10 to 12 minutes at 325°F.

This recipe has enough milk protein to complement both the peanut and wheat protein.

"Peanut Butter" Bread

3 loaves of 13 slices

one slice = approx. 3 g usable protein
7 to 9% of daily protein allowance

2½ cups warm stock
2 tbsp dry baking yeast
½ cup milk powder
½ cup peanut butter

¼ cup molasses
1½ tsp salt
6½ cups whole wheat flour
   divided, approximately
4 tbsp soy flour

Dissolve the yeast in the warm liquid. Add the milk powder, peanut butter, molasses, and salt. Blend well and stir in 4 cups of the whole wheat flour. This will be a wet "sponge"; let it rise about 1 hour or until it has risen quite high.

Stir the sponge down and stir into it 1½ cups more of whole wheat flour and the soy flour. Knead it until smooth and elastic, adding wheat flour if necessary. Let rise again until double in bulk (about 1 hour), punch down, knead again for a few minutes, and divide the dough into three parts. Put the loaves into oiled pans, let rise again till they are quite high, then bake at 350°F for about 40 minutes.

This bread rises high and makes a light and tasty loaf. Although the recipe has more wheat flour than fits the peanut-wheat-milk complementary proportions, the additional flour is complemented by the soy flour and the extra milk powder.

Spiced Peanut Loaf Cake

1 small loaf, 10 slices

one slice = approx. 4 g usable protein
9 to 11% of daily protein allowance

1 cup milk + 1 tbsp nonfat
  dry milk
1/2 cup peanut butter
1/2 cup honey
1/2 tsp salt
1 tsp cinnamon, ground
2 tsp baking powder

1/2 tsp nutmeg, ground
1/2 tsp cloves, ground
1/2 tsp fresh ginger, ground
1 3/4 cups whole wheat flour
1/2 cup each raisins and
  chopped nuts (optional)*

Blend milk, peanut butter, and honey in a blender. Add the salt, spices, and baking powder and blend again. Put the whole wheat flour in a small mixing bowl and pour about one-third of the liquid over it. Blend very gently with a wooden spoon, and continue adding the liquid. You want to stir gently to avoid developing any gluten in the flour so your cake will be tender. (Add the raisins and nuts) and pour into an oiled loaf pan, *or* fill gem or muffin wells two-thirds full. Bake the loaf 45 minutes to 1 hour, muffins about 30 minutes, or until they are golden brown like the color of peanut butter.

---

* The dried fruit makes this not-too-sweet cake more of a dessert. If you omit the fruit, you might add 1/3 cup peanuts and 1/2 cup sunflower seeds to create another complementary combination.

Spaghetti for Peanuts

4 servings

average serving = approx. 16 g usable protein
37 to 44% of daily protein allowance

2 cups dry broken spaghetti (whole wheat, if possible), cooked tender
2–4 tbsp butter
3 tbsp flour
1 tsp salt
1 tsp dry mustard
1/4 tsp pepper

2 cups buttermilk (or milk)
1/2 onion, chopped fine
3 drops hot pepper sauce
1/2 cup sliced black olives
1 cup grated cheddar cheese
1 cup chopped peanuts
1/3 cup bread crumbs

Melt butter and blend in flour, mustard, pepper, and salt. Add milk, onion, and hot sauce, stirring until thickened. Put half the spaghetti in a greased casserole with half the olives, cheese and peanuts on top. Repeat layers. Pour sauce over the top and then sprinkle with bread crumbs that have been moistened in melted butter. Bake at 350°F for 25 minutes.

Variation: Turn this spaghetti casserole into a cauliflower casserole by simply substituting cauliflower for the pasta and add 1 cup chopped green pepper.

19. Sesame Seeds* and Milk

Complementary Proportions

1¼ cups sesame seeds or 1½ cups sesame meal or ⅔ cup sesame butter	Slightly more than 1 cup skim milk or 4 tbsp nonfat dry milk (5½ instant)

Meat Equivalency Comparisons	
	Usable Protein Equivalent to:
A. If eaten separately:	
¼ cup nonfat dry milk	2 oz steak
1½ cups sesame meal	3 oz steak
	5 oz steak
B. If eaten together: 20% increase	
¼ cup nonfat dry milk + 1½ cups sesame seed meal	6 oz steak

* You may wish to substitute sunflower seeds. The same complementary effects would probably hold true. See complementary combination 5 for explanation.

Sesame-Nut Squares

12 squares

one square = approx. 4 g usable protein
9 to 11% of daily protein allowance

2 eggs, separated
2/3 cup honey
3 tbsp dry milk (4 tbsp
  instant)
1/4 cup whole wheat flour
1/4 tsp salt

1/2 tsp each, cinnamon and
  nutmeg
1 cup black walnuts,
  chopped
3/4 cup sesame seeds
2 tsp baking powder

Beat egg yolks until thick and yellow. Blend honey into yolks. Stir together the remaining ingredients and add to them the honey-yolk mixture. Mix well. Fold in the egg whites which have been beaten until stiff. Turn into oiled, long baking pan. Bake 30 minutes at 350°F. Served when still warm, these squares are light and delicate. Cooled, they are a little chewy but just as good.

Sesame Crisp Cookies

30 cookies

each cookie = approx. 2 g usable protein
5 to 6% of daily protein allowance

1/2 cup honey	1 1/4 cups oatmeal
1/2 cup oil	1 cup whole wheat flour
1 egg, beaten	1 tsp cinnamon, ground
1/4 cup milk	1/4 tsp salt
1/3 cup milk powder (1/2 cup instant)	3/4 cup sesame seeds
	1/2 cup raisins, chopped

Blend together honey, oil, and egg. Stir in remaining ingredients. Dough should be quite stiff. (Thin with milk or thicken with flour as necessary.) Drop batter by teaspoons onto oiled cookie sheet; flatten with the bottom of a glass which is dipped into cold water each time. Bake at 375°F 10 minutes.

There is enough milk powder called for to fill the sesame-milk proportions and still have enough left over to improve the protein quality of the flours.

Crunchy Granola

about 12 cups

1 cup = approx. 9 g usable protein
21 to 25% of daily protein allowance

½ cup vegetable oil
½–1 cup honey
1 tbsp vanilla
4 tbsp powdered milk (5½ instant)
2 tbsp brewer's yeast

1 cup wheat germ
1¼ cups sesame seeds
½–2 cups coconut shreds
1 cup rolled wheat
7 cups rolled oats

In a large saucepot heat together oil, honey, and vanilla until the mixture is very thin. Stir in the remaining ingredients in the order given, coating each one lightly with the honey mixture. The cereal can be toasted one of two ways: (1) Put all of the cereal in a large (9x13x2¼-inch) shallow pan, and place in cold oven. Turn heat to 350°F and watch for the browning to begin. Stir in the browned parts and check every 5 to 10 minutes, stirring to scrape sides and bottom of pan. Continue cooking until all of the cereal is deep golden brown. (2) Spread thin layers of the cereal on baking sheets and toast in a 225°F oven for about 1½ hours.

Granola is really a delicious way to start the day with milk, yogurt, nuts, and dried or fresh fruit. In this recipe, the milk powder complements the sesame seed. But to complement the grains, you will need to add milk or yogurt.

Sesame Seed Delight

18 pieces

one piece = approx. 3 g usable protein
7 to 8% of daily protein allowance

I cup sesame meal	½ cup grated coconut
4 tbsp dry milk (5½ instant)	¼ cup nut meal
¼ cup each butter and sesame butter	¼ cup honey, or more
	¼ cup raisins
½ cup toasted wheat germ	

Cream butters and blend with all of the remaining ingredients. Roll in 1- or 1½-inch balls. Chill several hours.

Variations: Delete grated coconut, add 2 tbsp vanilla extract or ¾ tsp mace, cinnamon, or cardamon.

20. Potatoes and Milk

Complementary Proportions

1 potato	1 cup skim milk
	or
	3½ tbsp nonfat dry milk (5 instant)
	or
	⅓ cup grated cheese

Meat Equivalency Comparisons	Usable Protein Equivalent to:
A. If eaten separately:	
⅔ cup nonfat dry milk	5 oz steak
3 large potatoes (about 2 lb)	1⅓ oz steak
	6⅓ oz steak
B. If eaten together: 7% increase	
⅔ cup nonfat dry milk + 3 large potatoes	6¾ oz steak

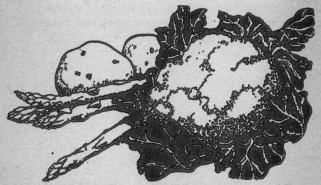

Cauliflower, Asparagus, Potatoes

253

Potato-Cauliflower Soup

about 2 quarts

1 cup = approx. 5 g usable protein
12 to 14% of daily protein allowance

1 cauliflower, cooked
3 potatoes, cooked and
 cubed
1 cup instant dry milk
4 cups stock, including the
 liquid from cooking the
 potatoes and cauliflower

2 tbsp butter
1½ tsp salt
½–1 cup grated or minced
 onion
optional vegetables*

Heat the stock in a large saucepan, and stir in the milk powder, butter, and salt. Put about a cup of this liquid in a blender with part of the cauliflower and potatoes (which have been cooked until very tender). Continue using liquid and blending the cauliflower and potatoes until all of the vegetables are smooth. You will probably have to empty and refill the blender jar several times. Return the soup to a saucepan and simmer it while you add the onion.

* While the soup is delicious as is, you can make it quite interesting by adding diced celery or carrots, or stirring in parsley, chives, or any fresh herbs. Serve with croutons or crumbled buttered toast.

Egg and Potato Bake

4–6 servings

average serving = approx. 12 g usable protein
28 to 34% of daily protein allowance

3 medium potatoes, cooked
and sliced

3 eggs, hard-boiled and
thinly sliced

2 tbsp butter

1 cup milk (or buttermilk)

Worcestershire sauce

1 cup cheese, grated
cheddar

1 tsp salt

pepper to taste

1/4 pound fresh mushrooms

wheat germ, raw

2 tbsp flour

In a saucepan, melt the butter, stir in the flour, then add the milk and cook slowly until thickened. Add Worcestershire sauce to taste and the salt and pepper. Stir in the grated cheese.

In an oiled casserole layer: ½ of the sliced potatoes, ½ of the eggs, ½ of the cheese sauce. Repeat. Top the final layer of sauce with the mushrooms which have been sliced. Sprinkle with wheat germ and bake at 350°F for 20 minutes.

Potato Latkes

2–3 servings

average serving = approx. 11 g usable protein
26 to 31% of daily protein allowance

½ onion, cubed
1 large potato, cubed with skin
2 tbsp whole wheat flour
2 tbsp chopped parsley

2 eggs
salt and pepper
5 tbsp instant dry milk
oil for frying

In an electric blender blend eggs, onion, and potato cubes. Then add and blend salt and pepper to taste, whole wheat flour, parsley, and powdered milk. Using this batter, fry like small pancakes in hot oil. Brown both sides well. Top with apple sauce, yogurt, or soft cheese.

This is a quick and easy supper dish which you can vary by omitting the dry milk and serving with cheeses or yogurt as above.

Ginger Snappy Potatoes

4–6 servings

average serving = approx. 10 g usable protein
23 to 28% of daily protein allowance

5 medium potatoes,
  boiled in the skin
1 cup stock (from boiling
  the potatoes)
10 tbsp instant dry milk
  (slightly less than ⅔ cup)

2–3 tbsp grated fresh
  ginger
3 tbsp butter
1 cup cheese, grated
salt to taste

Cool the potatoes and peel only the skin without removing any of the potato beneath it. Mash the potatoes in a saucepan and add the stock which has been mixed with the powdered milk. Put over a very low heat, and add the ginger and butter, stirring until the butter is melted. Salt to taste. Remove from the heat and stir in the grated cheese. (It doesn't have to melt completely.) Serve with lightly steamed broccoli or greens.

If you are fond of ginger, you can add up to ¼ cup either grated or sliced.

C. Menu Ideas

Breakfast Suggestions

Hot Breakfast

	Percent of Daily Protein Allowance
juice	
1 hot, buttered Orange-Sesame Muffin	12–14%
1 egg	14–17%
	26–31%

½ grapefruit	
2 small Cornmeal-Soy Waffles	30–36%
hot tea	

favorite fresh fruit with	
⅓ cup (dry) oatmeal cooked with	7–8%
2 tbsp soy grits	14–17%
½ cup milk	8–10%
	29–35%

Cold Breakfast

melon slice	
Crunchy Granola with	21–25%
½ cup milk	8–10%
	29–35%

"Quicky" rice cereal

⅔ cup cold cooked rice (left-over) with 2 tbsp toasted sesame seed, raisins, brown sugar, and ½ cup milk or buttermilk	14–17%
	8–10%
	22–27%

Lunchtime Suggestions

Salad Lunches

	Percent of Daily Protein Allowance
Cold Gallentine	14–17%
Garbanzo-Cheese Salad	19–22%
	33–39%

Macaroni Salad Ricotta served on bed of lettuce with wedges of tomato and	16–20%
½ hard-boiled egg	7–8%
Sesame Crisp Crackers	9–11%
	32–39%

Soup Lunches

Mediterranean Lemon Soup	14–17%
Middle Eastern Tacos	23–28%
cold apple cider	
	37–45%

chilled tomato juice	
Potato-Cauliflower Soup	12–14%
"Wine, Bread, Cheese, and Thou"	14–17%
	26–31%

Sandwich Lunches

hot tea	
2 slices Boston Brown Bread each with	14–16%
⅛ cup ricotta cheese mixed with	12–14%
chopped nuts and raisins	3–4%
	29–34%

Percent of Daily
Protein Allowance

sandwich of toasted whole wheat bread with	5–6%
Soy-Sesame-Peanut Spread	7–8%
cheese (1 oz)	14–17%
sliced tomato and lettuce	
	26–31%

Dinner Suggestions

Dinners with a Foreign Flavor

"Italian" Dinner:

tossed green salad	
Minestrone con Crema	23–28%
Sesame Eggplant Parmesan	28–34%
favorite melon with sherbet scoop	
	51–62%

"Indian" Dinner:

crisp salad of diced celery, pineapple, carrots, mandarin oranges, and apples with yogurt	
Sweet and Pungent Vegetable Curry over Mixed Grains	35–42%
Cottage Cheese Cake	21–25%
	56–67%

"Mexican" Dinner:

avocado dip (guacamole) with corn chips	
Tostadas	26–31%
Fine Fruit Salad (dessert)	12–14%
	38–44%

*Percent of Daily
Protein Allowance*

or	
Con Queso Rice	39–47%
broccoli with lemon butter	5–6%
Cornbread	14–17%
applesauce	
	58–70%

"Oriental" Dinner:

miso (soy paste) base soup	
Sukiyaki over rice	23–28%
tea	
Sesame Crisp Cookies (2)	10–12%
	33–40%

Other Favorites

Cream of Tomato and Rice Soup	12–14%
Walnut Cheddar Loaf	30–36%
green peas with new onions	7–8%
apple-spice cake with spice frosting	16–20%
(see Chameleon Spice Cake)	
	65–78%

Soybean Croquettes with cheese sauce	
served over mixed grains	32–39%
green beans with sautéed mushrooms	2–3%
Indian Pudding with yogurt topping	28–34%
	62–76%

	Percent of Daily Protein Allowance
Savory Onion Quiche	28–34%
Tabouli (Lebanese Salad)	9–11%
oven-warmed pumpernickel bread	2–3%
Tangy Rice-Sesame Pudding	14–17%
	53–65%
tossed green salad	
Spaghetti for Peanuts	37–44%
fresh steamed asparagus	3–4%
fruit cup with Sesame Dream Bar	5–6%
	45–54%
Caesar salad	
Gourmet Curried Eggs on Toast (or Rice)	37–44%
steamed fresh broccoli	5–6%
raspberry sherbet with Sesame Nut Squares	9–11%
	51–61%
lightly marinated cucumber and tomato slices	4–5%
Sesame Rice Fritter-Puffs with cream sauce	16–20%
steamed spinach or other greens	3–6%
hot buttered Pineapple-Corn Muffins	7–8%
	32–42%

Herbs

Appendix A

Basic Cooking Instructions
Beans, Grains, Nuts and Seeds

In order to avoid repetition among the recipes, here are instructions for preparing the basic ingredients often called for.

A. Cooking Beans

1. Regular Cooking: Wash beans in cold water, and soak overnight in three times the volume of water; *or* bring the beans and water to a boil, cover tightly, and let sit for 2 hours. Simmer the beans, partially covered, adding water if necessary, for about 2 hours, depending on the type of bean and the consistency you want. If you want to mash or puree the beans, you will want to cook them until they are quite soft.

2. Pressure Cooking: A pressure cooker is a real advantage in cooking beans as well as grains. Since the foods cook so much quicker, a meal doesn't require as much forethought! Pressure cooking also gives you a more tender bean. Soaking or precooking, as in method 1, saves a little time, but with pressure cooking it really is not necessary. Bring the washed beans and three to four times their volume in water to a boil in the cooker. Cover and bring to 15 pounds pressure. Cook beans for 25 to 45 minutes. Cool immediately. Don't attempt to cook split peas or any bean that tends to foam in a pressure cooker, or you may find yourself with a clogged cooker and a big mess.

3. Roasting: Cook beans by one of the above methods for a firm bean. Spread the beans on a lightly oiled baking sheet. Sprinkle with salt, if desired, and bake at 200°F for about 1 hour until they are well browned. When they are hot, they will be crunchy outside and tender inside. When they are cool they will be hard and crunchy throughout. You can also roast the beans in a lightly oiled frypan over medium heat on top of the stove. Stir constantly. Roasted soybeans can be eaten alone, or when chopped, or ground in a blender. They make a garnish to be sprinkled on a variety of dishes, or use them when nuts or nutmeal is called for.

4. Making Soybean Curd (Tofu): Soy curd can be purchased in many parts of the country. If it is not available to you, you might wish to try making it. *The Natural Foods Cookbook* has several recipes. I'm not including a recipe here because my single attempt failed. However, the "failure" served as a base for delicious salad dressing made by blending spices, herbs, onions, garlic, and avocado.

B. Cooking Grains

1. Regular Cooking: Wash the grains in cold water. Bring stock or water, equal to twice the volume of the grains, to a boil (for millet or buckwheat use three times the volume). Put in the grains, bring to a boil again, lower heat and simmer (covered) for 30 to 45 minutes until all of the liquid is absorbed.

2 Pressure Cooking: In the pressure cooker follow the same method but instead of simmering the grain, bring to 15 pounds pressure and cook for about 20 minutes. Cool under cold water when cooking time is up. You may wish to vary the amount of water to create the texture of grain you prefer. If you have trouble with sticking, here's the trick I use: Place about 1 inch of water in the bottom of the pressure cooker. Put the grain into a stainless steel bowl that will fit easily into the pressure cooker (with plenty of room between the top of the bowl and the lid of the pressure cooker). Add water to the level of about ¾ inch above the level of the grain. Put the bowl inside the pressure cooker, cover, and begin cooking. This method is also handy when I need to cook both grains and beans at the same time, but separately. I merely put the small stainless steel bowl inside the pressure cooker. I then place the beans with adequate water around the outside of the bowl and the grains inside the bowl.

3. Sautéing: This method is most frequently used in cooking bulgur wheat and buckwheat groats, but can be used with any grain to achieve a "nuttier" flavor. Wash the grains and put in a dry saucepan or pressure cooker over low heat. Stir until dry. Add just enough oil to coat each kernel. Sauté the grains, stirring constantly, until all of the grains are golden. Stir in boiling water or stock (amounts given in 1 above) and bring the mixture to a boil. Cover and simmer 30 to 45 minutes; or, if using a pressure cooker, bring to 15 pounds pressure and cook 20 minutes. Cool cooker immediately.

C. Cooking Nuts and Seeds

1. To Roast Whole Seeds or Nuts: Place in a dry pan and roast over medium flame until desired brownness. Or spread them on a baking sheet and toast them in a 200°F oven. Use the seeds whole, or grind them in a blender, a few at a time, or with a mortar and pestle. Add salt if desired.

2. To Roast or Toast Seed or Nut Meal: Buy the meal, or, to make it yourself, grind the seeds or nuts in a blender. Then roast the meal in a dry pan, stirring constantly, adding salt, if desired. Or spread the meal on a baking sheet, and bake at 200°F, stirring often. (You can also grind small quantities of whole grains in your blender.)

3. Nut and Seed Butters: It is easy to make your own fresh nut and seed butters if you have a blender. From whole roasted or raw seeds or nuts: Grind as for meal, adding a little oil to "start" the butter. Continue adding as many nuts or seeds as your blender can handle. From roasted or raw nut or seed meal: Stir a little oil, and honey, if desired, into the meal, and you will have creamy nut or seed butter.

Peas

Appendix B

Calorie/Protein Comparisons

Listed here is the number of calories you have to consume in order to get *1 gram of usable protein* from selected foods. Foods having more than 60 calories per gram of protein are excluded. See text for explanation.

Sources of Protein Listed in Increasing Order of Calories	No. of Calories per Gram of Usable Protein	Sources of Protein Listed in Increasing Order of Calories	No. of Calories per Gram of Usable Protein
1. Seafood*		Tuna, bluefin	8
Haddock	5	Salmon, humpback	8
Cod	5	Bass, striped	8
Halibut	6	Mackerel, Pacific	9
Shrimp	6	Tuna, canned in oil	9
Squid	6	Shad	11
Lobster	6	Oysters	11
Rockfish	6	Perch	13
Flounder or sole	6	Herring, Pacific, canned in oil	14
Herring	8	Sardines, Atlantic canned in oil	22
Clams	8		
Carp	8		
Swordfish	8		

*Raw unless otherwise indicated.

Sources of Protein Listed in Increasing Order of Calories	No. of Calories per Gram of Usable Protein	Sources of Protein Listed in Increasing Order of Calories	No. of Calories per Gram of Usable Protein
2. Nutritional Additives		Spinach	18
Egg white, dried	9	Asparagus	18
Tiger's Milk	8	Cauliflower	18
Brewer's yeast		Green limas	19
(nutritional yeast)	12	Turnip greens	20
Baker's yeast	15	Chard	20
Wheat germ	19	Mustard greens	22
3. Dairy Products		Collards	24
Dried egg white	6	Mung bean sprouts	25
Cottage cheese,		Peas	25
uncreamed	7	Okra	27
Creamed cottage		Artichoke	28
cheese	10	Corn	37
Nonfat milk and		Potato, white	60
buttermilk	12		
Dried nonfat milk		**5. Legumes (Dry Seed)**	
solids	12	Tofu (soybean curd)	15
Whole egg	14	Soybeans	20
Ricotta cheese	14	Mung beans	25
Parmesan cheese	16	Broadbeans	28
Edam cheese	16	Split or whole peas	30
Plain yogurt from		Cowpeas	
skim milk	18	(Blackeye peas)	33
Swiss cheese	19	Limas	33
Cheddar cheese	23	Kidney beans (red)	39
Whole milk	23	Common white beans	39
Camembert cheese	24	Garbanzos	
Blue mold cheese	24	(chickpeas)	40
Roquefort cheese	26	Lentils	47
Plain yogurt from			
whole milk	27	**6. Flour**	
Yogurt, sweetened,		Soybean flour,	
w/fruit	30	defatted	11
4. Fresh Vegetables		Soybean flour, low fat	12
Soybean sprouts	12	Soybean flour, full fat	18
Mushrooms	14	Gluten flour	23
Broccoli	16	Rye flour, dark	34
Brussel sprouts	16	Whole wheat flour	41
Kale	17	Buckwheat flour, dark	43
		Barley flour	58

Sources of Protein Listed in Increasing Order of Calories	No. of Calories per Gram of Usable Protein	Sources of Protein Listed in Increasing Order of Calories	No. of Calories per Gram of Usable Protein
Cornmeal, whole ground	80*	Brown rice	69*
7. Grains, Cereals, and Products		**8. Nuts and Seeds**	
Wheat germ	19	Pumpkin and squash seeds	32
Wheat bran	24	Pignolia nuts	36
Wheat, whole grain (hard red spring variety, w/most protein)	40	Sunflower seeds	40
		Peanuts	49
		Peanut butter	51
Oatmeal	41	Cashews, roasted	55
Whole wheat bread	43	Whole sesame seeds	57
Buckwheat pancake	46	Black walnuts	60
Pumpernickel	47	Pistachio nuts	60
Rye bread and whole grain rye	48	Brazil nuts	88†
Egg noodles, macaroni, and spaghetti	50	**9. For Comparison: Meat and Poultry**	
		Chicken fryer, breast	7
Cracked wheat cereal	52	Turkey, roasted	9
Bulgur, from hard red winter wheat	53	Lamb, lean only	10
		Porterhouse steak, lean and marbled	14
Cornbread with whole ground meal	55	Hamburger	15
		Pork loin chop, lean and fat	18
Millet	60	Lamb rib chop, lean, marbled, and fat	32
Barley	60		

*Notice that brown rice and cornmeal exceed the 60-calorie limit. See discussion for explanation.

†Brazil nuts also exceed the calorie limit but are included because of their very high content of sulfur—containing amino acids, a rare virtue among plant foods.

Appendix C
Protein Cost Comparisons

Protein Sources Listed in Increasing Order of Cost	Cost per 43.1 g Usable Protein*	Protein Sources Listed in Increasing Order of Cost	Cost per 43.1 g Usable Protein*
1. Dairy Products:		Ricotta cheese (@ 53¢/lb)	62¢
Dried nonfat milk solids (@ 39¢/lb)	10¢	Blue mold cheese (@ $1.16/lb)	75¢
Cottage cheese from skim milk (@ 31¢/lb)	19¢	Parmesan cheese (@ $2.14/lb)	82¢
Buttermilk (@ 19¢/qt.)	29¢	Yogurt from skim milk (@ 44¢/lb)	$1.52
Whole egg (@ 63¢/doz)	33¢	Camembert cheese (@ $1.98/lb)	$1.56
Whole milk, nonfat milk (@ 26¢/qt)	44¢	**2. Legumes (Dry Seed)**	
Dried egg whites (@ $3.66/lb)	51¢	Soybeans, soygrits, and flour (@ 33¢/lb)	15¢
Swiss cheese (@ $1.05/lb)	53¢	Cowpeas (Blackeye peas) (@ 16¢/lb)	16¢
Cheddar cheese (@ $1.13/lb)	62¢	Split peas (@ 19¢/lb)	19¢

*43.1 g of usable protein is the daily allowance for the "average" American male weighing 154 pounds. "Usable" protein means that the protein has been reduced by the NPU score to the level that the body can actually use. Formula for calculating price per 43.1 g of usable protein:

$$\frac{price}{\% \ protein \ X \ \# \ oz \ X \ NPU \ (as \ a \ \%)} \ X \ 1.54 = cost \ per \ 43.1 \ g \ usable \ protein$$

Protein Sources Listed in Increasing Order of Cost	Cost per 43.1 g Usable Protein*	Protein Sources Listed in Increasing Order of Cost	Cost per 43.1 g Usable Protein*
Lima beans (@ 23¢/lb)	20¢	Macaroni (@ 25¢/lb)	37¢
Common white beans (@ 23¢/lb)	26¢	Brown rice (@ 21¢/lb)	38¢
Chickpeas (garbanzos) (@ 25¢/lb)	27¢	Gluten flour (@ 68¢/lb)	41¢
Lentils (@ 23¢/lb)	31¢	Wheat bran (@ 42¢/lb)	46¢
Kidney beans (@ 28¢/lb)	31¢	Barley flour (@ 28¢/lb)	46¢
Mung beans (@ 43¢/lb)	31¢	Buckwheat flour, dark (@ 37¢/lb)	46¢
Black beans (@ 39¢/lb)	40¢	Egg noodles (@ 37¢/lb.)	47¢
		Millet (@ 35¢/lb)	60¢

3. Grains, Cereals, Products

Whole wheat flour (@ 19¢/lb)	21¢	Cornmeal, whole ground (@ 32¢/lb)	63¢
Rye flour, dark† (@ 22¢/lb)	22¢	Whole wheat bread (@ 38¢/lb)	66¢
"Roman Meal" (@ 25¢/lb)	27¢	Rye bread (@ 39¢/lb)	69¢
Whole grain wheat, hard red spring (@ 27¢/lb)	27¢	"Super-cereal"†† (@ 59¢/8 oz)	$1.06

4. Seafood

Oatmeal (@ 28¢/lb)	28¢	Turbot (@ 59¢/lb)	28¢
Spaghetti (@ 23¢/lb)	34¢	Squid (@ 39¢/lb)	28¢
"Protein Plus" (@ 45¢/lb)	35¢	Herring (@ 45¢/lb)	31¢
Bulgur, red (@ 27¢/lb)	35¢	Cod (@ 75¢/lb)	33¢
Barley, pot or scotch (@ 22¢/lb)	37¢	Swordfish (@ 79¢/lb)	34¢
		Perch (@ 59¢/lb)	37¢
		Tuna, canned in oil (@ 96¢/lb)	48¢
		Catfish (@ 79¢/lb)	54¢

*43.1 g of usable protein is the daily allowance for the "average" American male weighing 154 pounds. "Usable" protein means that the protein has been reduced by the NPU score to the level that the body can actually use. Formula for calculating price per 43.1 g of usable protein:

$$\frac{price}{\% \text{ protein } X \text{ } \# \text{ oz } X \text{ NPU (as a \%)}} \times 1.54 \text{ az cost per 43.1 g usable protein}$$

†Notice: other types with less protein would be relatively more expensive per gram of protein.

††Included to show that brand-name high-protein cereals may not necessarily be good "protein buys."

Protein Sources Listed in Increasing Order of Cost	Cost per 43.1 g Usable Protein*
Sardines, Atlantic, canned in oil (@ 85¢/lb)	56¢
Salmon (@ 89¢/lb)	62¢
Oysters (@ 69¢/lb)	76¢
Crab, in shell (@ 59¢/lb)	84¢
Clams, soft, in shell (@ 59¢/lb)	$1.41
Shrimp, canned wet pack (@ $3.79/lb)	$3.03

5. Nutritional Additives

Wheat germ (@ 47¢/lb)	27¢
"Tiger's Milk" (@ $1.98/lb)	46¢
Brewer's yeast (nutritional yeast) (@ $1.20/lb)	54¢
Baker's yeast (@ $1.60/lb)	87¢

6. Nuts and Seeds

Peanut butter (@ 61¢/lb)	54¢
Raw peanuts (@ 66¢/lb)	57¢
Sunflower seeds or meal (@ 90¢/lb)	62¢
Sesame seeds or meal (@ 71¢/lb)	69¢
Peanuts (@ 92¢/lb)	76¢

Protein Sources Listed in Increasing Order of Cost	Cost per 43.1 g Usable Protein*
Pumpkin and squash kernels (@ $1.80/lb)	$1.00
Raw cashews (@ $1.31/lb)	$1.30
Brazil nuts (@ $1.00/lb)	$1.33
Black walnuts (@ $1.96/lb)	$1.82
Cashews (@ $2.41/lb)	$2.19
Pignolia nuts (@ $3.56/lb)	$2.23
Pistachio nuts, in shell (@ $2.61/lb)	$5.20

7. Meats and Poultry

Hamburger, reg. grd. (@ 63¢/lb)	51¢
Chicken breast w/bone (@ 69¢/lb)	62¢
Pork loin chop med. fat, w/bone (@ $1.09/lb)	$1.15
Porterhouse steak choice grade, w/bone (@ $1.58/lb)	$1.67
Lamb rib chop, choice grade, w/bone (@ $1.49/lb)	$1.81

*43.1 g of usable protein is the daily allowance for the "average" American male weighing 154 pounds. "Usable" protein means that the protein has been reduced by the NPU score to the level that the body can actually use. Formula for calculating price per 43.1 g of usable protein:

$$\frac{price}{\% \ protein \ X \ \# \ oz \ X \ NPU \ (as \ a \ \%)} \ X \ 1.54 \ az \ cost \ per \ 43.1 \ g \ usable \ protein$$

Appendix D

Sample Calculation: Conversion of Nonmeat Protein into Beef Equivalent

Legumes and Rice

I. Eaten separately—no complementarity of protein quality
   A. Legumes
      1. 1½ cups legumes = 61.5 grams protein
      2. Adjusting for protein quality:
         Protein Efficiency Ratio (PER*) = 1.65
            (for legumes eaten alone)
         Protein Efficiency Ratio = 2.30
            (for beef)
         1.65/2.30 X 100 = 72%, i.e., the approx. amount of
         protein available to the body from legumes is only
         72% of that available from beef
         Thus, 72% of 61.5 grams = 43.7 grams
         of protein equivalent to beef
      3. Converting protein equivalent to meat equivalent:
         Only 25% of beef is protein; therefore, 4 X 43.7
         grams = 174.8 grams or about 6¼ oz of beef
   B. Rice
      1. 4 cups of rice = 59.2 grams protein
      2. Adjusting for protein quality:
         Protein Efficiency Ratio = 1.91
            (for rice eaten alone)
         Protein Efficiency Ratio = 2.30
            (for beef)
         1.91/2.30 X 100 = 83%; 83% of 59.2 grams =
         49 grams of protein equivalent to beef
      3. Converting to meat equivalent: 4 X 49 = 196 grams
         or about 7 oz of beef

*PER is the gain in weight of the growing experimental animal divided
by the weight of protein consumed. It is accepted by nutritionists as a
good measure of protein quality. PER correlates highly with NPU, a term
which is explained in the text.

II. Eaten together—complementarity increases protein quality

A. 1½ cups legumes = 61.5 grams
   +
   4 cups rice = 59.2 grams
   } = 120.7 grams

B. Adjusting for protein quality:
   2.52 = approx. PER of legumes and rice
   eaten together (in proportions given)
   2.30 = PER of beef
   2.52/2.30 X 100 = 110%
   110% of 120.7 grams = 132.2 grams protein
   equivalent to beef

C. Converting protein equivalent to meat equivalent:
   132.2 X 4 = 529 grams or about 19 oz. beef

Appendix E

Pesticide Residues in the American Diet 1964–1968

Item	Percent of Diet*	Percent of Chlorinated Pesticides Item Contributes to Diet	Average Content DDT, DDE, and TDE, ppm†
1. Dairy products (8-13% fat)	31	16	0.112
2. Meat, fish and poultry (17-23% fat)	10	36	0.281
3. Grains and cereals	16	9	0.008
4. Potatoes	7	2	0.003 (DDT & DDE only)
5. Leafy vegetables	3	4	0.036
6. Legumes	3	2	0.026
7. Root vegetables	3	1	0.007 (DDE only)
8. Fruits	21	25	0.027
9. Oils, fats, shortening	3	4	0.041
10. Sugar and adjuncts	3	1	—

*Excludes beverages which are generally pesticide-free: based on typical diet of 16 to 19-year-old males.

†Based on averages of data presented for five cities: Boston, Kansas City, Los Angeles, Baltimore, and Minneapolis, these chlorinated pesticides comprise two-thirds of the total; they are the only ones for which data are sufficiently complete to permit tabulation.

Source for pesticides in diet: R. E. Duggan and G. Q. Lipscomb, "Dietary Intake of Pesticide Chemicals in the U.S. (II), June 1966—April 1968,"

and *Pesticides Monitoring Journal,* 2; 153-162, 1969; "Pesticide Levels in Foods in the U.S. from July 1, 1963—June 30, 1967, *Ibid.,* 2:2—46, 1968.

Source for DDT, DDE, TDE levels: P.E. Corneliussen, "Pesticide Residues in Total Diet Samples (IV)," *Ibid.,* 2: 140—152, 1969.

Appendix F
Whole Wheat Flour Compared to White Flour

	Composition of Whole Wheat Flour (per 100 g or 3½ oz)		White Flour		Enriched White Flour	
1. Protein	13.3	g	10.5 g	79%	10.5 g	79%
2. Minerals						
Calcium	41	mg	16 mg	39%	16 mg	39%
Phosphorous	372	mg	87 mg	23%	87 mg	23%
Iron	3.3	mg	0.8 mg	24%	2.9 mg	88%
Potassium	370	mg	95 mg	26%	95 mg	26%
Sodium	3	mg	2 mg	67%	2 mg	67%
3. Vitamins						
Thiamin	0.55	mg	0.06 mg	11%	0.44 mg	80%
Riboflavin	0.12	mg	0.05 mg	42%	0.26 mg	216%
Niacin	4.3	mg	0.9 mg	21%	3.5 mg	81%

Composition of All-Purpose White Flour Compared to Whole Wheat Flour

Appendix G

Brown Rice Compared to Other Types of Rice

	Composition of Brown Rice (per 100 g or 3½ oz)			Composition of Other Rice						
				White Rice		Enriched White Rice		Converted Rice (Enriched)		
1. Protein	7.5	g		6.7	g	90%	6.7	g	90%	7.4	g	99%
2. Minerals												
Calcium	32	mg		24	mg	75%	24	mg	75%	60	mg	190%
Phosphorous	221	mg		94	mg	43%	94	mg	43%	200	mg	90%
Iron	1.6	mg		0.8	mg	50%	2.9	mg	180%	2.9	mg	180%
Potassium	214	mg		92	mg	43%	92	mg	43%	50	mg	70%
Sodium	9	mg		5	mg	56%	5	mg	56%	9	mg	100%
3. Vitamins												
Thiamin	0.34	mg		0.07	mg	21%	0.44	mg	130%	0.44	mg	130%
Riboflavin	0.05	mg		0.03	mg	60%	0.03	mg	60%	0.03	mg	60%
Niacin	4.7	mg		1.6	mg	34%	3.5	mg	74%	3.5	mg	74%

Appendix H

Sugars, Honey and Molasses Compared

Composition (per 100 g or 3½ oz)

	White Sugar (Granulated)	Brown Sugar (Beet or Cane)	Molasses (Third Extraction or Blackstrap)	Honey (Strained or Extracted)	Maple Sugar
Minerals	mg	mg	mg	mg	mg
Calcium	0	85	684	5	143
Phosphorus	0	19	84	6	11
Iron	0.1	3.4	16.1	0.5	1.4
Sodium	1.0	30	96	5	14
Potassium	3.0	344	2927	51	242
Vitamins					
Thiamine	0	0.01	0.11	trace	—
Riboflavin	0	0.03	0.19	0.04	—
Niacin	0	0.2	2.0	0.3	—

Source: "Composition of Foods," Agriculture Handbook, No. 8, U. S. Dept. of Agriculture. Values given vary in other sources.

Notes:

Part I

1. *The World Food Problem*, A Report of the President's Science Advisory Committee, Vol. II, May 1967, p. 249.
2. Donald Patton, *The United States and World Resources*, D. Van Nostrand Co., Inc., Princeton, N.J., 1968, p. 112.
3. A. M. Altschul, "Combatting Malnutrition: New Strategies Through Food Science," *Plant Foods for Human Nutrition, 1* (No. 3):152, 1969.
4. Calculated from *National and State Livestock-Feed Relationships*, U.S. Department of Agriculture, Economic Research Service, Statistical Bulletin No. 446, Feb. 1970, p. 76.
5. Calculated from *Feed Situation*, Feb. 1970, U. S. Department of Agriculture, Economic Research Service, p. 8.
6. Max Milner, "General Outlook for Seed Protein Concentrates," in: *World Protein Resources*, A. Altschul (ed.), Advances in Chemistry, Series 57, Washington, D.C., 1966, p. 53.
7. *Feed Situation*, August, 1969, p. 21.
8. *The World Food Problem, op. cit.*, p. 338.
9. Calculated from the following sources:
   a) The World Food Problem, op. cit., p. 338;
   b) National and State Livestock-Feed Relationships, op. cit., p. 76.

10. F. Wokes, "Proteins," *Plant Foods for Human Nutrition, 1* (No. 1):32, 1968

11. C. C. Bradley, "Human Water Needs and Water Use in America," *Science, 138*:489, 1962.

12. N. W. Pirie, *Food Resources Conventional and Novel,* Penguin Books, Baltimore, Md., p. 110, 1969.

13. Roy M. Kottman, "Animal Agriculture Meeting Its Critical Issues Head-On," in: *Proceedings: Sixteenth National Institute of Animal Agriculture,* 1966, p. 34.

14. Don Paarlberg, "The Potential Impact on Animal Agriculture of a Changing U.S. Policy as a Result of the World's Food-Population Ratio," *Ibid,* p. 7.

15. Quentin M. West, "Revolution in Agriculture, New Hope for Many Nations," in: *Food for Us All,* Yearbook of Agriculture 1969, U.S. Department of Agriculture, p. 83.

16. Ernest F. Hollings, *The Case Against Hunger,* Cowles Book Co., Inc., New York, 1970, pp. 83, 84, 104.

17. Telephone interview with Mr. James Clawson, Extension Animal Scientist, Animal Science Extension, U. of California, Davis, May 12, 1970.

18. Kottman, *loc. cit.,* pp. 37-38.

19. *Fisheries of the U.S., 1968,* U.S. Department of Interior, U.S. Fish and Wildlife Service, Bureau of Commercial Fisheries, CFS No. 5000, p. 30.

20. *U.S. Foreign Agricultural Trade by Countries,* Fiscal Year 1968, U.S. Department of Agriculture, Economic Research Service, p. 30.

21. "Major Uses of Land and Water in the U.S., Summary for 1959," Agricultural Economic Report No. 13, Farm Economics Division, Economic Research Service, U.S. Department of Agriculture, p. 2.

22. A. I. Virtanen, "Milk Production of Cows on Protein-Free Feed," *Science, 153*:1603–14, 1966.

23. *The World Food Problem, op. cit.*

24. *U.S. Foreign Agricultural Trade by Countries, op. cit.,* p. 55.

25. *Cereal Science Today, 15* (No. 4):120, 1970.

26. *Fisheries of the U.S., 1968, op. cit.,* p. 30.

27. S. J. Holt, "The Food Resources of the Ocean," *Scientific American, 221*:178–94, 1969.

28. *Environmental Science and Technology, 4* (No. 12): 1098, 1970.

29. Calculated from the following sources:
    a) *Food and Agriculture Organization Production Yearbook*, Vol. 22, 1968;
    b) *Rubber Statistical Bulletin, 23* (No. 12), Sept. 1969.

30. *The State of Food and Agriculture 1965*, Food and Agriculture Organization (U.N.), Rome, p. 22.

31. William A. Albrecht, "Physical, Chemical, and Biochemical Changes in the Soil Community," in: *Man's Role in Changing the Face of the Earth*, William L. Thomas, Jr. (ed.), The University of Chicago Press, 1956, p. 671.

32. Georg Borgstrom, "Food and Ecology," *Ecosphere, The Magazine of the International Ecology University, 2* (No. 1):6, 1971.

33. R. E. Duggan and G. Q. Lipscomb, "Dietary Intake of Pesticide Chemicals in the United States (II), June 1966–April 1968," *Pesticides Monitoring Journal, 2*: 162, 1969.

34. H. L. Harrison, O. L. Loucks, J. W. Mitchell, D. F. Parkhurst, C. R. Tracy, D. G. Watts, V. J. Yannacone, Jr., "Systems Studies of DDT Transport," *Science, 170*:503–8, 1970.

35. P. E. Corneliussen, "Residues in Food and Feed: Pesticide Residues in Total Diet Samples (IV)," *Pesticides Monitoring Journal, 2*:140–52, 1969.

36. Sheldon Novick, "A New Pollution Problem: Federal Officials Comment," *Environment, 11*:8, 1969.

37. G. C. Decker, "Chemicals in the Production of Food," in: *Proceedings: Western Hemisphere Nutrition Congress, 1965*, p. 131.

38. *Third World Food Survey*, Freedom from Hunger Campaign, Basic Study No. 11, Food and Agriculture Organization (U.N.), Rome, 1963, p. 20.

39. *The State of Food and Agriculture 1969,* Food and Agriculture Organization (U.N.), Rome, pp. 162, 181.
40. *The World Food Problem, op. cit.,* p. 74.
41. J. C. Abbott, "Protein Supplies and Prospects: The Problem," in: *World Protein Resources, op. cit.,* pp. 6–8.
42. Thelma J. McMillan, "Your Basic Food Needs: Nutrients for Life, Growth," in: *Food for Us All, op. cit.,* p. 257.
43. *Livestock and Meat Situation,* November 1969, U.S. Department of Agriculture, Economic Research Service, p. 20.
44. Rex F. Daly, "Food Enough for the U.S. A Crystal Ball Look Ahead," in *Food For Us All, op. cit.,* p. 92.
45. *Recommended Dietary Allowances,* 1968 Revision, Food and Nutrition Board, National Research Council, National Academy of Sciences, Washington, D.C.
46. *The World Food Problem, op. cit.,* p. 317.
47. Abbott, *loc. cit.,* p. 1.

Part II

48. A. M. Altschul, *Proteins, Their Chemistry and Politics,* Basic Books, Inc., N.Y., 1965, p. 118.
49. *Protein Requirements,* Report of a Joint FAO/WHO Expert Group, Food and Agriculture Organization, Rome, 1965, pp. 35–38.
50. Helen A. Guthrie, *Introductory Nutrition,* The C. V. Mosby Co., St. Louis, 1967, p. 53.
51. *Protein Requirements, op. cit.,* p. 43.
52. *Evaluation of Protein Nutrition,* National Academy of Sciences, National Research Council, Pamphlet No. 711, Washington, D.C., p. 16.
53. *Canadian Bulletin on Nutrition,* Dietary Standard for Canada, 1964, p. 24c.
54. *Protein Requirements, op. cit.,* p. 22.
55. R. J. Williams, "We Abnormal Normals," *Nutrition Today,* 2:19–23, 1967.
56. *Protein Requirements, op. cit.,* p. 32.
57. *Amino Acid Content of Foods and Biological Data On*

Proteins, Food and Agricultural Organization of the U.N., Rome, 1970.

58. A. M. Altschul, 1965, *op. cit.,* p. 115.
59. A. G. Long and F. Wokes, "Vitamins and Minerals in Plants," *Plant Foods for Human Nutrition, 1* (No. 1): 43–50, 1968.
60. Guthrie, *op. cit.,* pp. 141, 194, 230, 239, 245, 221.
61. *Ibid.,* pp. 122, 123, 130.
62. *Ibid.,* p. 262.
63. G. Clement, C. Giddey, R. Menzi, *Journal of the Science of Food and Agriculture, 18*:497 (1967).
64. *The State of Food and Agriculture 1964, op. cit.,* p. 105.
65. A. M. Altschul, 1965, *op. cit.,* pp. 111–12.
66. *Protein Requirements, op. cit.,* p. 48.
67. *Amino Acid Content of Foods, op. cit.*
68. R. Bressani, "Formulated Vegetable Mixtures," in: *Proceedings: Western Hemisphere Nutrition Congress,* 1965, p. 88.
69. Ellen H. Liu, and S. J. Ritchey, "Nutritional Value of Turkey Protein," *Journal of the American Dietetic Association, 57*:39–41, 1970.
70. Jean Mayer, "Nutritional Aspects of Preventative Medicine," in: *Preventative Medicine,* D. W. Clark, B. MacMahon (eds.), Little, Brown and Co., Boston, 1967, p. 200.

Sources for Tables

1. *Amino Acid Content of Foods and Biological Data on Proteins,* Food and Agricultural Organization of the U.N., Rome, 1970.
2. Bowes, A., and F. Church, *Food Values of Portions Commonly Used,* 10 ed., revised by C. F. Church and H. N. Church, J. B. Lippincott Co., Phila., 1966.
3. *Composition of Foods,* Agriculture Handbook No. 8, Agricultural Research Service, U.S. Dept. of Agriculture, 1963. (Available at U.S. Govt. Book Stores.)
4. Orr, M. L., and B. K. Watt, *Amino Acid Content of Foods,* Home Economics Research Report No. 4, U.S. Dept. of Agriculture, 1957.

5. *Protein Requirements,* Report of a Joint PAO/WHO Expert Group, Food and Agriculture Organization, Rome, 1965.

Background Sources

1. Aykroyd, W. R., and Joyce Doughty, *Legumes in Human Nutrition,* Food and Agriculture Organization, Nutritional Studies No. 19, 1964.
2. Borgstrom, Georg, *The Hungry Planet,* Collier Books, N.Y., 1967.
3. ————, *Too Many,* The Macmillan Co., N.Y., 1969.
4. Courtenay, P. P., *Plantation Agriculture,* Frederick A. Praeger, N.Y., Washington, 1965.
5. *Economic Impact of Coffee,* World Coffee Information Center, 1968.
6. *Evaluation of Protein Quality,* National Academy of Sciences, National Research Council, Washington, D.C., 1963.
7. Houston, D. F., and G. O. Kohler, *Nutritional Properties of Rice,* National Academy of Sciences, Washington, D.C., 1970.
8. *International Action To Avert the Impending Protein Crisis,* United Nations, Sales No. E, 68 XIII 2., 1968.
9. Jalée, Pierre, *The Third World in World Economy,* The Monthly Review Press, N.Y., 1969.
10. Kon, S. K., *Milk and Milk Products in Human Nutrition,* Food and Agriculture Organization, U.N., Nutritional Studies No. 17, Rome, 1959.
11. May, Jacques, *Ecology of Malnutrition in Middle Africa,* Hafner Publishing Co., N.Y., London, 1965.

Recommended Cookbooks

1. *El Molino Best,* Tested Recipes from El Molino Kitchen, El Molino Mills, 1955.
2. Hunter, Beatrice Trum, *The Natural Foods Cookbook,* Pyramid Books, N.Y., 1961.
3. Light, Louise, *In Praise of Vegetables,* Scribner and Sons, N.Y., 1966.
4. Richmond, Sonya, *International Vegetarian Cookery,* Arco Publishing, N.Y., 1965.

Write Your Own Recipes Here

Recipes

Recipes

Recipes

Recipes

Recipes

INDEX

How to Avoid Poisoning Ourselves
Daily With the Food We Eat

THE BASIC BOOK OF ORGANIC GARDENING

Edited by Robert Rodale

Now the long-established *Organic Gardening* Magazine and Ballantine Books have produced an original book to guide the unknowledgeable gardener to healthy living through gardening in nature's own way—without pesticides and artificial fertilizers. All the basic information is here:

> What organic gardening is.
>
> Where organic gardening supplies can be obtained.
>
> How to prepare the soil, compost, mulch, etc.
>
> Why gardening organically is essential to the protection of the environment.

An *Organic Gardening*®/Ballantine Book $1.25

YOU ARE WHAT YOU EAT

FROM BALLANTINE'S NATURAL LIVING SERIES